Vanishing Hardwoods in Rural America

Myron Finkbeiner

AuthorHouse™
1663 Liberty Drive, Suite 200
Bloomington, IN 47403
www.authorhouse.com
Phone: 1-800-839-8640

© *2010 Myron Finkbeiner. All rights reserved.*

No part of this book may be reproduced, stored in a retrieval system, or transmitted by any means without the written permission of the author.

First published by AuthorHouse 2/19/2010

ISBN: 978-1-4490-5097-9 (e)
ISBN: 978-1-4490-5099-3 (sc)

Printed in the United States of America
Bloomington, Indiana

This book is printed on acid-free paper.

Contents

Foreword vii

Introduction xi

1. Some Old High School Gyms Find New Life – Indiana 1
2. Ahead of its time – Nampa, Idaho 7
3. John Wooden and the World's Largest High School Gym – Martinsville, Indiana. 15
4. Panthers' Pride – Augusta, Kentucky 21
5. Home Of a Ghost – Oxford, Kansas 27
6. Bedlam in a Bandbox – Flagler, Colorado 31
7. The Old Barn – Welch, Oklahoma 37
8. Welcome to the Old West – Monument, Oregon 43
9. The Tale of Two Gyms – Wheatland & Forrest, New Mexico 51
10. The Little Town That Could – Weskan, Kansas 59
11. A Small Town, a Tiny Gym, and a Hero – Geddes, South Dakota 65
12. Hoosiers, It's Not – Brooklyn, Washington 71
13. Improbable Heroes – Bellfountain, Oregon 79
14. Hardwood Glory, '60s Style – Wishek, North Dakota 87
15. Terry Teagle's Landmark – Broaddus, Texas 95
16. A Changing Landscape On the Hi-Line – Chester, Montana 101
17. Bearden's Bears Den is Mighty Cozy – Bearden, Oklahoma 109
18. Round Ball in a Round Gym – New Providence, Iowa 113
19. They Played in Dirt Before They Played On Wood – Farwell, Nebraska 119
20. Big Dreams Are Realized In Small Towns – Alamo, Nevada 127
21. Hoosier Madness – Cannelton, Indiana 137

Acknowledgements 143
Epilogue 145
Contributors' Biographies 149
Notes 153

VANISHING HARDWOODS IN RURAL AMERICA
Foreword

Small towns in America continue to vanish, swallowed up by economic times, and abandoned for the lure of urban life. Farming is no longer profitable in the many regions of the US and the job markets have dried up. People move to cities to find work. Consequently, school enrollments decrease. It is no longer feasible to administer school functions, let alone field athletic teams. The communities consolidate while school districts build bigger regional schools.

Case Study: Collyer, Kansas. Travelling the Interstate through Kansas we saw far out on the horizon what appeared to be a spire, perhaps of a church. As we drew closer, it became clear that it was a Catholic Church, sitting alone against a vast backdrop of prairie land, as a lone sentinel. Why was a structure of this kind sitting out in the middle of nowhere? We pulled off the freeway to find the answer.

The community, or what was left, looked like a ghost town. There were vacancies, run-down businesses, dilapidated housing, and streets crumbling away. We drove past what looked like a rather large school. It too, was vacant with weeds growing up, broken windows everywhere, doors and walls falling apart, all indicating it's been years since children played on her playgrounds and students filled its hallways.

Finally, my wife and I arrived at a magnificent church structure standing alone in the midst of desolation. How sad! We walked to the front door and found it open. As we entered it demanded a respectful silence and we immediately felt a strange power. We wanted to fall upon our knees as an act of reverence. We could only imagine the thousands over time who had worshiped in this house of God. What would the walls say if they could only speak?

Through the back door came a little lady who greeted us warmly. After some introductions and letting us know she was the caretaker, she informed us of the church's history. She told it had prevailed through economic hard times and how it had stood the test of time. Fourth and fifth generation German Catholics still called it their parish. The church was the only building still functioning in this small town. What little population remains, they drive to larger communities for food and services. The school children are bused to Quinter, a consolidated school some 25 miles up the freeway. She finished by saying, "We've gone the same way so many other small towns in Kansas have gone."

Along with the transformation of America from rural to an urban society, there has been a transformation of America's moral economy. In other words, the rural life that once shaped most people's character is nearly gone. There remains the question that must be asked. What does the death of a community cost its members? And what does it cost the country? With the demise of rural schools and its gymnasiums, one can see the concern.

Collyer, Kansas, represents thousands of communities across America. These stories are the motivations for writing, "Vanishing Hardwoods." This scenario is being played out all over rural America and with it comes a storyline that needs to be told. With the decline of small communities comes also the decline of schools and with it an All- American institution, the high school gymnasium. In my opinion, rural gyms are as much a part of America as baseball, Chevrolet and apple pie.

My high school playing days in Idaho spawned my interest in diminutive gyms. "I remember going to Kuna High School, whose gym doubled as the school's library. As we arrived to dress down, students were pushing portable book shelves from the gym to storage areas in the hallway. At Greenleaf, I suffered a shoulder injury, when I plowed into a wall that served as the end line. Middleton High School's gym was so small, that all four walls marked the out-of-bounds lines. On one jump ball, a teammate's foot went crashing through the hardwood." With these experiences, one would think playing under those circumstances should be forgotten. Now years later, those experiences become even more fascinating. Could they be duplicated in other rural communities?

There just aren't many of the old high school gymnasiums that were built in the 1920s, '30s and '40s still in use as varsity facilities. They have gone the way of under-hand free throws and two-handed set shots. Some are being used by elementary and junior high teams or converted into community centers. Basketball gyms built prior to the fifties have a different feel than those built today. They were smaller and more intimate. The gyms built today are spacious and designed for comfort, so the intimacy and the emotions flooding from that atmosphere have been lost. Though many of those "cracker boxes" are no longer in existence, some are still around if one takes time to locate them.

This book was written for the sole purpose of finding these gyms and telling their stories. As I crisscrossed the country to find these historic relics, I discovered many were unique or unusual in one way or another. However, all had a common thread, a special charm and fascination. Each had a tale to tell.

These old gyms I found were more than wooden courts for basketball. They were sites for many venues. Most have a stage at one end for assemblies where countless number of graduates received their diplomas and where many homecoming queens were crowned.

Most of the gyms were vastly undersized, with odd court dimensions and peculiar characteristics unique to each facility. All possessed, however, a certain quality of ambiance and atmosphere. They were places to go back in time. They were cozy, intimate, neighborly- like, and a gathering place for the entire community to watch their local high school teams play on Friday nights.

Only a few ticks remain on the old game clocks. Just enough time is left to visit some of the old treasures. Hopefully, readers of "Vanishing Hardwoods" will be taken back in time and relive some precious days of yore.

Myron Finkbeiner

Introduction

I remember the cracker box gyms in rural America, with hoops hanging on the end walls; pillars extending onto the playing floor and a pot-bellied stove in one corner. I remember the small town rivalries that were played on a cold, rainy, Willamette Valley night. If you are the type of person who has watched "Hoosiers," at least a dozen times, then this book is for you.

I played and coached in many of them. They were all-purpose structures, having the capacity to host a wide variety of community events. I remember running into end walls and being dumped into the wooden bleachers bordering the playing floor. The entire atmosphere was one of closeness. Everywhere we played, the home team had an advantage.

Many of these quaint old gyms still exist and are being used. But, sorry to say, in recent years in an effort to modernize and because of the downturn in the economy resulting in consolidation, many are being torn down.

The author, Myron Finkbeiner, a former high school and college basketball coach, decided before it's too late it's time to search out these old relics; to photograph them; to talk with the old coaches, players and community fans; and collect information that can yet be documented.

His labor of love has resulted in a book entitled, "Vanishing Hardwoods in Rural America." Simply, it's a collection of essays on grass-roots basketball and inspirational stories that can come only from small-town America.

"Vanishing Hardwoods" will be an interesting read for every fan of basketball. I thoroughly enjoyed reading it, as it brought back memories of my high school playing days at Creswell, Oregon. It was a place I spent a good portion of my youthful days. Fortunately, the small gym is still there and remains a focal point of the community. Creswell is a basketball town…. always has been and always will be.

Mark Few,

Basketball Coach, Gonzaga University

SOME OLD HIGH SCHOOL GYMS FIND NEW LIFE IN INDIANA

"In my research for this book, a common thread prevailed throughout… the demise of rural schools and gyms due to consolidation, and their subsequent survival from the wrecking ball which are being provided by proactive communities. Kyle Neddenriep did a piece for the Indystar.com that overviews the decline and survival of these historical gymnasiums in the state of Indiana. The article provides examples of communities that have been hard hit by consolidation and what some concerned citizens are doing to keep the vintage gyms from biting the dust. I placed the article at the beginning of the book as it will serve as a framework and foundation for the remaining chapters."

The high, dusty windows throw light into the darkness of the sleepy Wayne County community of Economy. Outside the white, barnlike structure, a familiar sound cuts through the bitterly cold night: the pounding thud, thud, thud of a basketball against hardwood floor.

Stand there a minute, shoes covered in snow, and imagine what's inside. There would be the student cheer block; farmers in overalls lining the perimeter of the court; young men and women sitting on planks above the bleachers, eating popcorn and hurling insults at referees.

All that is gone. Economy, Indiana, oldest wooden gym in the State …Credit: Mike Fender

Once the heartbeat of a community, the Economy gym now stands empty except for Wednesday nights like this, when community members do their best to bring it back to life.

Look hard enough and you can still find these old gyms, remnants of a bygone and uniquely Hoosier era. They were home to the Ladoga Canners, the Mecca Arabs, the Pinnell Purple Dragons, the Bridgeton Raccoons, and the Stilesville Tigers. Now they are elementary schools, community centers, fire stations, private businesses, churches, libraries. Some, like the one in Sandusky, are homes. Others, sadly, are embarrassing eyesores.

The stories they could tell. Built mostly from the 1920s to the 1950s, before the antiseptic, multipurpose "athletic facilities" of today, each had its own unique feature, such as the crow's-nest scorer's table in Bloomfield, the out-of-bounds walls in Mecca (it wasn't long enough for end lines) and the wrap-around balcony in Harrisburg.

Most had this in common: They were packed for every game.

"That's why these gyms mean so much to people," said Phyllis Beers, a 1954 graduate of Green Fork High School, where the gym is now used to park fire trucks. "Going to basketball games was the thing to do. People have a fondness for those days."

Look hard enough and you can still find these hidden gems. But don't wait too long.

It has been 50 years since the School Corporation Reorganization Act caused sweeping consolidation of school districts across the state. In 1959, there were 724 basketball-playing high schools. This year, there are 402.

Once the students left, there was no more reason to keep many of the gyms. Others were razed in the name of progress, or finances. More are on the chopping block. The Rush County towns of Arlington, whose gym dates to 1939, and Milroy (1928) are building new elementary schools, and the current schools and adjoining gyms could be demolished.

"It's sad," said Priscilla Winkler, a 1955 Arlington graduate. "But it would be difficult to keep the gym financially."

Some have survived because it would have cost too much to tear them down and build new ones. New Market kept its gym, built in 1957, after the high school consolidated into Southmont in 1971. A new elementary school was built around it.

Many other gyms, in places such as Amo, Covington, Fillmore and Pine Village, have avoided the wrecking ball the same way.

Still others have been used as community centers, sometimes made available for rental. Such is the case at Indiana's most famous former high school gym in Knightstown. The home court of the fictional Hickory Huskers in "Hoosiers," the 1922-built gym likely would have been torn down if not for the movie. Now it draws 10,000 to 15,000 visitors a year.

In Fountain County, the former home of the Veedersburg Green Devils is owned by a nonprofit group of local residents who have raised more than $100,000 to refurbish the gym and school, known as the "Hub Civic Center."

"We didn't want this place to become dilapidated," said Jim Robinson, who saw that happen at his alma mater, Richmond Township.

Jim Dickey and John Glancy of the tiny Blackford County village of Roll know the feeling. Sixteen years ago, they bought the Roll gym, which was built in 1938 as part of the Works Progress Administration projects of the 1930s and '40s.

The men, who played on the Roll Red Roller teams of the early 1950s, hold on to the gym like an old friend. Though it's rented out occasionally, there is no money to be made. There is only the satisfaction of knowing that it's still there.

"When they took the school away, the town died," Dickey said. "That gym is about all that's left."

Dickey estimates that of the 30 or so gyms he played in as a high school student, only three or four remain. Some that still stand, do so barely.

The old Dover school, a few hundred yards from Western Boone High School, is a mess. Windows are busted out, and the roof is leaking.

The Alamo gym, built in 1941 and once a source of pride in the Montgomery County town, is for sale by a private owner. Charlie Bowerman, a 1957 graduate and member of the Indiana Basketball Hall of Fame, remembers it fondly.

"You hate to see the way it looks now," said Bowerman, who lives in Oklahoma. "We had some great memories in that place."

For other gyms, survival has come in myriad forms. Newport's 1925 jewel is part of a public library. Pay $1, and you can use it for an hour. In Kingman, the 1936 gym is part of the Community Christian Church Center.

Josh Reitzel has operated his rental company out of the 1938 Stilesville gym for five years. The 1953 Coal Creek Central gym is a warehouse. Classic gyms in Lebanon (1931) and Crawfordsville (1941) were remade as part of a health club. The 1923 Noblesville gym is used by the Boys & Girls Club.

All had their imperfections. There were dead spots on the court; cramped seating; and poor ventilation. The Economy floor is 61 feet long, 23 feet short of high school regulation.

The warts only made them more revered.

"We played in gyms so small you couldn't even shoot a high-arcing shot," said Bill Townsend, who coached at Fountain City in the 1950s. "Those places were great."

"It was entertainment in those little towns back then. You didn't have to be a parent or grandparent to go to the games. You could have put on a catfight instead of a basketball game, and the same people would have come to watch."

Those people are now the same ones hoping to preserve history in places that haven't seen a high school game in 50 years.

"I'd cry my eyeballs out if they ever tore this place down," said Bud Tutterow, a 1960 Economy graduate. "I'd buy it myself and give it to the township if it ever came to that."

Less than two weeks ago, Anderson voted to keep its huge "Wigwam" gym despite evidence that it was no longer financially viable.

"The gyms will always have that connection to the community," said Jon Detweiler, who helped lead a recent restoration of the 1953 Williamsburg gym. "People don't want them to go."

AHEAD OF ITS TIME

"My first chapter had to be Central gym in my home town of Nampa, Idaho. I played on this hallowed hardwood all through my growing-up years. Of all the gyms I researched for this book, Central Gym had the qualities you would look for in a complete facility. Gyms of the future could learn from the architects and builders of Central Assembly."

The Idaho State Championship was on the line. The Nampa Bulldogs were up by five at halftime. In addition to winning the coveted crown, the Bulldogs were also attempting to go for a record no previous team had ever accomplished…. an undefeated season. We had 28 wins in a row and one half of a game to go to make it 29.

One problem, the captain and leading scorer, an All-American schoolboy player, Wayne Blickenstaff, was saddled with four fouls. In the locker-room, previous to the opening of the second stanza, Coach Babe Brown gave substitute Finkbeiner a nod and asked, "Myron, are you ready to take Wayne's place in the starting lineup and help this team win State?"

Stunned and for a loss of words, I contemplated the question for a moment when my mind went back a year to when I and two teammates transferred to Nampa High School from a small private school. Comments from my peers at the new school were not complimentary. "Fink, you're stupid to transfer… you'll never make the team!" Those comments stuck in my craw and served as a powerful force to succeed at this higher level. Remembering those words, I answered the call from the coach with an enthusiastic, "Yes, I can do it!"

I grew up in a small rural community in southwest Idaho. The city of Nampa began as a small railroad town in 1880, and today it's still a major hub for Union Pacific Railroad. An early day citizen was Colonel William Dewey, a man who made a fortune mining gold in Silver City. To get the ore rich in silver and high in the Owyhee Mountains, Dewey built his own railroad that made its way down the steepest of slopes, across miles of sagebrush plains to eventually find its way to a tiny community named after an early day notorious Indian, Chief Nampuh. Today, Nampa is often referred to as the industrial and agricultural center of Idaho and as the state's "Friendliest" city.

It is appropriate for the opening chapter to describe the gym most familiar to me. Nampa's Central Assembly Auditorium in Nampa was the venue where I began and ended my active playing career.

Central Assembly building, Nampa, Idaho …Credit: Author

My earliest recollection of playing at Central was in an eighth grade tournament. Our grammar school, part of Northwest Nazarene College, was too small to field a team from one grade, so the remaining teammates came from the 6th and 7th grades.

Northwest Nazarene College had a high school on its campus, which served as a training ground for its students intending to enter the teaching field. The academy, as it was called, had a long tradition in winning basketball games. Very few teams in the area scheduled the small private school for fear of losing to the Trojans. The academy played as an independent team and often played in Central as a preliminary game to Northwest Nazarene.

In 1949, after my junior year at the academy, I and teammates, Jay and Mickey Dean transferred to the larger and more prominent, Nampa High School. It was a good move, as the Bulldog team with three new players and led by legendary coach, Babe Brown, became the most successful team in Idaho School Boy history. The Central gym, with the capacity 1,800, was sold out for nearly every Bulldog game.

Following high school graduation, Northwest Nazarene College recruited me as a student-athlete. The short trip across town again took me and my playing abilities to Central Assembly Gymnasium. For sixteen straight years I played on Central's hardwood, scoring over 1,200 points in 105 games, while recording 72 wins. Now that Central is no longer used by the College or Nampa High, the playing records at Central should never be broken. "I'm indebted to the experiences gained while playing in that fabled gymnasium."

We tend to believe basketball arenas, as pictured on university campuses, have been around for eons. Not so! Gyms in the early days had fixed bleachers, better to crowd more fans into smaller spaces. There were exceptions … one being McArthur court on the University of Oregon campus. Still in use today by the Ducks, this storied old arena, built in 1925, is the forerunner to today's basketball palaces. In 2001, *SPORTING NEWS* magazine named it the best gym in America for its history, character and atmosphere. Don't tell that to the visiting teams playing there today, as they call "The Pit" an absolutely horrible facility for play. Duck fans wouldn't change a thing, for they know their beloved team has a huge home court advantage.

Another exception was my home town gym. In 1935 the Nampa School District designed a basketball facility that would be more than a playing court, including theater seating in a horseshoe configuration, with a seating capacity of 1800. For cultural events, throw in 750 folding chairs on the floor and you have seating for 2,550 people. Even the name, Central Auditorium, spoke to its diversity. Over the years it was the site for political rallies, church services, commencement programs, concerts and drama productions. Athletically, it played host to a variety of events. The two Idaho universities played their annual game there. As the largest school facility, state tournaments were conducted frequently. I remember standing in long lines to watch high school boxing matches. The internationally famous Harlem Globetrotters and the House of David annually came to Nampa. Those were the days of Goose Tatum, Meadowlark Lemon and Marques Haynes. To see them in Nampa, Idaho was a real treat.

Few high schools in America during the 30's and 40's had gyms with theater-type seating. Most had bleachers on one side with the players sitting in folding chairs on the opposite side. As basketball popularity increased in the 40's, the courts took on a new look. This look included permanent bleachers on both sides and elevated 6 to 10 feet above the playing service---the purposes being to keep spectators off the floor, to protect the shiny playing surfaces, and to avoid confrontations between fans and players. Next, roll-a-way bleachers came, as schools continued looking for innovative multi-purpose uses for their gymnasiums. Rolling the bleachers against the wall provided more floor space and opportunities to convert gyms into auditorium settings.

Old-timers who played here in the '50s re-create their playing days
...Credit: Author

Today, 85 years later, Central gym, other than having the stage enclosed, remains the same. The rectangle wood backboards still hang in place. It does not rock like it once did, with a noisy crowd and a pep band blaring out the Bulldog fight song. Today it's quieter and home to a middle school crowd and a less than active recreation basketball leagues. I'm sure the local participants today are unaware of the long, rich history the old gym has provided Nampa natives.

To borrow a phrase from a popular TV program, if the floor could talk, we would hear stories emanating from the gym. One would be about a successful basketball coach, J.A. "Babe" Brown. The legendary mentor guided teams at Nampa High from 1947-1957. Fifty years later, Nampans still talk about the 1950 undefeated team that went 29-0, and marched its way to a State Championship, never having a close game. Many of the players went on to successful college careers, some even became All-Americans. Somewhere in a school's trophy case is a tie under glass, that reads, "The tie that never saw defeat." It was worn by Babe at each of the 29 games.

Northwest Nazarene College was forced to use Central as its venue for home games, as visiting teams hesitated to come to Nampa to play the Crusaders in their ancient cracker box. On one occasion, Western Montana journeyed to Nampa to play on a Friday night on campus and was soundly defeated by 25 points. The following night the two teams squared off at Central where Montana turned the tables by outscoring the hosts by 32 points. A turnaround of 57 points! To bring it into perspective, it would be like playing one night in a hayloft, followed the next night with a game in the "Fabulous Forum."

A game during my sophomore year will go down in history as being the most bizarre basketball game ever played in Central. Cross-county rival, the College of Idaho, came to town led by a pair of African-Americans, not commonly seen during those days in Idaho. R.C. and Elgin came to the Caldwell College to play football, but quickly learned that basketball was their sport.

The game between the rivals was played before a packed house, with the Crusaders as a decided underdog. The evening got off to an unfriendly start. As the Coyotes paraded on to the floor, R.C. placed a phonograph player on the stage, which burst forth with, "Sweet Georgia Brown." NNC's big center, Carlyle Dean, took offense to the incident, as this was his home floor, and angrily yanked the cord from the wall. Coach Monty Lee stepped between Carlyle and R.C. before a scuffle became apparent.

The contest was evenly played throughout the first half, when in the late moments, Elgin picked up his fourth foul. What happened next would make ESPN's "50 All-time Stupid Remarks." I was the team captain and the obvious person Elgin came to with his strange request, and begged, *"You are the captain ... please go to the referee and have him change that last call. After all, the fans came to watch me play!"* I stood there dumbfounded and couldn't believe what I just heard. Of course I didn't heed his request! It reminded me of a story played out in 1915. The great Jim Thorpe playing with the Canton Bulldogs faced Knute Rockne in a controversial game between the Bulldogs and Massillon, Ohio. As Rockne told the story, he tackled Thorpe for a loss. "You mustn't do that, Rock," Thorpe said to the future Notre Dame coaching legend. "These fans paid to see old Jim run. Be a good guy and let old Jim run." On the next play, Thorpe's knee smashed into Rockne's head as Thorpe broke for a Touchdown. "That's a good boy, Rock," Thorpe said, coming back to check on his would-be tackler, "you let old Jim run."

In the second half, the referees didn't listen to Elgin's request as he fouled out with 17 minutes remaining. The NNC fans went delirious, believing now the game was in the bag. Not so, C of I managed to win without their star. Unfortunately for NNC, R.C., with his tremendous jumping ability, blocked a last second shot attempt by NNC's Carlyle Dean. Could it be R.C. jumped a bit higher because of the pulled plug earlier in the evening?

Now the rest of the story... R.C. Owens, during his NFL career was known for his jumping abilities. He once blocked a field goal by jumping up at the cross bar knocking the attempted kick harmlessly to the ground. Y.A. Tittle and R.C. invented and perfected the "Alley-Oop", a rainbow spiral that dropped from the clouds just as the leaping Owens rose like a rocket to cradle it. For ten years he made spectacular catches for the San Francisco 49ers. Elgin left C of I after only one year, transferring to Seattle University, where he had an All-American career. You'll know him best as Elgin Baylor who forged an NBA All-star career. *Sports Illustrated* named him one of the fifty greatest players in the last century. He later became GM for the Los Angeles Clippers. One final comment: when Baylor fouled out early in that historical game, he managed only nine points.... more than likely the only time in his career that he didn't reach the double figures.

Today, Central Auditorium "stands like a rock." Its concrete walls and appearance haven't changed. Old-timers from Treasure Valley frequently drift into the almost sacred building to relive the sights, sounds and even the smells of yesteryears. They recall a time when the pace of life was slower, when the auditorium was the center of community life, and where dreams were born. Yes, Central was ahead of its time. Nampans are indebted to those who had the foresight to construct a facility to serve a community for almost a century. May Central gym never vanish, but remain as a tribute to those who ran up and down its hardwood, and to the thousands of fans who witnessed countless numbers of games.

One game will never be forgotten. On March 16, 1950, the blue and red clad Bulldogs recorded a record setting 29-0 season, on their way to a State

Championship, helped in part by a non-descript sixth man. The transfer silenced his detractors.

One Sticky Defense

Buffalo Gap, South Dakota, held an invitational basketball tournament in the early years, with an afternoon session, followed by a pancake feed, and then an evening session. My father, Ole Lather, was head coach at New Underwood and his team was scheduled to play one of the evening games. The gym was extremely small, and also served as the school's hot lunch room, so between sessions, tables and chairs were moved onto the playing floor for the pancake feed. As might have been expected, maple syrup was spilled on the floor, and despite the efforts of the janitor to clean it up, it was still present at game time.

Dad, who used a man-to-man press in his team's game against Hill City, swears that the bottoms of his players' shoes were sticking to the floor when they came into contact with the syrup, and that's where the phrase, "sticky man-to-man defense" originated.

Submitted by Deny Lather, Watertown, SD

JOHN WOODEN AND THE WORLD'S LARGEST HIGH SCHOOL GYM

"As a young basketball coach attempting to learn the trade, I would invariably go to the Master, Coach John Wooden. Later in my career, I came to know him in an intimate way and will forever cherish our friendship. Fortunately, in recent days I ran into Elmer Reynolds, retired sportswriter from Martinsville, Indiana, where Coach Wooden's childhood home was. Elmer has known Wooden since their growing-up days. Without a doubt, he has more knowledge than anyone else of Martinsville's fabled gym where John Wooden had his All-State high school career. It is only appropriate that Elmer share his thoughts on Martinsville and the gym that Wooden made famous."

It was Thursday night, February 21, 1924, on the eve of our nation's observing President George Washington's Birthday that a thirteen year old farm boy named John Wooden would have been in his central Indiana small community home.

On this bitter cold, Midwestern winter night, John was completing his 8th grade homework assignment for his Centerton, Indiana teacher, principal, coach and lifelong mentor, Earl Warner. The family was gathered around a black pot-belly stove listening intently as their father Joshua Hugh Wooden read aloud by the light of a coal-oil lamp. The elder Wooden, an honest, hard working farmer, with a great appreciation for knowledge, poetry, classic books (especially "The Good Book") and a quality education, would read Tennyson, Shakespeare, Poe and the Bible to his adoring family.

On that cold Indiana winter night, just eleven miles south, an event was taking place that ultimately impacted not only Indiana, but the entire nation in the decades that followed. Two special trains left Shelbyville bound for Martinsville carrying 1500 Shelby County residents. The trains were making their way through the countryside to deliver their passengers to a momentous event: a high school basketball game.

Martinsville Gymnasium dedication game, February 21, 1924 ...
Credit: Artesian Yearbook

Even in those days Indiana was basketball crazy, but it wasn't simple hoops action that drew these fans to the Mineral City. And, while Martinsville would go on to win the state championship that year, the Shelbyville loyalists were not attracted by a powerhouse opponent .... Martinsville had a mediocre 13-7 season and certainly didn't look like champions before the tournament. Nor were the fans, as one would guess, traveling to get a glimpse of Martinsville's John Wooden ... he was not a star in 1924, and had not yet begun high school.

No, Shelbyville residents made their pilgrimage to see a building, the new Martinsville High School Gymnasium. Nationally syndicated columnist Robert Ripley would later feature the gym in his popular "Believe It Or Not" column. Martinsville had the foresight to erect a gymnasium to seat 5,200 fans. For a community of 4,800 to build a facility that size, struck

Ripley as a "believe it or not!" The local newspaper billed it as the "Biggest Gym in the World."

On this blustery February evening, a jam-packed gym was overflowing with basketball fanatics. Old-timers, who were in attendance for the dedication of Martinsville's new basketball palace, claimed people were literally hanging from the rafters. Many fans from rival Shelbyville were turned away because of the full house.

The home team suffered the loss, but the fact that Martinsville now had a world-class gym which would accommodate large crowds, overshadowed the feeling of regret because of the defeat. The next day, the local newspaper summarized the reaction of most locals:

"The big gym was packed to capacity and the cheering throng, the noise of the bands, and the brilliant display of school colors presented a scene never to be forgotten by those present."

Looking back to that historical night, which took place just miles from John Wooden's home, one wouldn't have foreseen that in just three years, a young Wooden would lead his Martinsville High School team to a State Championship.

The game took on added significance, not only for the announced attendance, the largest crowd ever to witness a schoolboy game, but to hear words of admonition from the Secretary of the Indiana High School Athletic Association. His message was important to that time and equally vital for today's general public. A.I. Treater said the following, "Martinsville can make out of this gym just what they want to make of it. It can be an aid to the making of better citizens, and as such, to the community... clean athletics, honest dealings, clean sportsmanship, and the building of character. Do away with all that is unclean. Make the gymnasium a laboratory for good citizenship and it will be worth it to Martinsville all that it has cost in time and money."

It wouldn't be long until basketball frenzy hit Martinsville High. Was it because of the new basketball court or because a new family moved into town? From a tiny dirt court in Centerton, came a future schoolboy sensation, with the name, John Wooden, known around the area as "Pert" as in "impertinent." To John, the Martinsville court, with its polished floor and modern bright lights, was like a little piece of heaven. Even the basketballs were round.

The Woodens came to Martinsville in John's sophomore year, after his Dad lost the farm and found work at the Home Lawn Sanitarium, one of the local spas whose artesian waters and treatments drew visitors from around the world.

Basketball was King in Indiana, but not in the Wooden home. Joshua Hugh Wooden made sure education was the top priority in his house. Even so, young John found enough practice time on the court to become a member of one of the best teams in Indiana.

Coach Wooden with his ten-time NCCA championships always preached the importance of self-control. He didn't practice what he preached as a young player. In his recent book, "My Personal Best," co-authored with Steve Jamison, he tells of an incident during his sophomore year that certainly shaped his future philosophy:

> *"During my sophomore year I got into a fight during practice with one of the starters, a big guy who occasionally used dirty tactics. We went at it hard until Coach Curtis came over, broke up the fight, and told me to apologize for starting it. I felt the other player was in the wrong – tripping me intentionally—and refused to say I was sorry, even though he claimed it was an accident. I didn't believe it. Finally, I got so worked up that I ripped off my jersey; took off my shoes, socks, and trunks; and threw them down in front of Coach Curtis. Then I stalked off the court. How he kept from laughing as I headed to the locker room nearly naked, I don't know.*
>
> *Fortunately, Glenn Curtis understood human nature pretty well. After letting me think about it a few days, he saw me in the hallway and said, 'Johnny, let's forget about what happened the other day and get back to practice this afternoon.'"*

John Wooden and his Martinsville Artesians had a great 3-year run. In those days, Indiana's state championships had only one division. Small rural high schools went up against the large city schools. That made Martinsville accomplishments even more incredible. In 1926, the Artesians advanced to the finals and in 1927 they won it all, defeating much larger Muncie Central.

It was in 1928 that Wooden remembers best, even though it didn't turn out well for his team. Again quoting "My Personal Best," Coach Wooden remembers:

> *"In the final seconds of the 1928 state championship, with us leading by one point, Muncie Central's Charlie Secrist flung a desperation underhand shot from half-court that literally went up to the rafters and came down straight through the hoop. It was impossible.*
>
> *Here's how impossible it was: in my forty years of coaching at Dayton High School, South Bend Central, Indiana State, and UCLA, I never saw anyone make that shot again. But I did see it once – Saturday night, March 17, 1928. In our locker room afterwards, the Artesians, stunned and almost grieving, sat on the benches holding towels over their faces as they wept. The last-second shot had been crushing, and all of the players just quietly lowered their heads and cried. All but one.*
>
> *I couldn't cry. The loss hurt me deeply, but I knew I'd done my best. Disappointed? Yes. Devastated? No. Dad taught us on the farm, 'Don't worry about being better than somebody else, but never cease to be the best you can be.' I had done that."*

The young John Wooden earned a basketball scholarship at Purdue, where he played under the great Ward Lambert. Much of Wooden's later coaching philosophy was learned while playing for Coach Lambert. Wooden's respect for Lambert grew over the years and came to realize his ability to transform individuals in a positive way. Wooden would later remark, "For me, he is the model of what a great coach and teacher can be."

**Glenn Curtis Memorial Gym, Martinsville, Indiana ...
Credit: Chip Keller**

After an All-American career at Purdue, Coach Wooden with his young bride, Nell, accepted a high school coaching position in Dayton, Kentucky. His career got off to a rough start and in fact, Coach Wooden said, "I was a terrible coach in the beginning. I was quick to criticize and slow to commend." To add insult to injury, Dayton journeyed to Martinsville for a game against the Artesians. In front of a packed house, maybe the biggest crowd ever to see a game in the gym where John had been an all-state player, his Green Devils lost 27-17. His coaching record at Martinsville still stands at 0-1!

Martinsville has honored John Wooden with a statue and a street name. Another obvious landmark is Wooden's home on Jefferson Street. While these landmarks of Wooden's youth might be overlooked by many local residents, the coach himself is not forgotten. The greatest monument to John R. Wooden might be the old gym where he started his career. While modern basketball palaces dwarf Martinsville's 1924 gym, the facility remained the city's primary hoops venue well into the 1970s. Thanks to community outcry by local sport enthusiasts, the gym survived the 1979 wrecking ball that demolished its accompanying 1915 high school, and received an interior makeover that allowed it to take on its current role as a middle school gym. Despite its makeover, from the outside it looks virtually the same as it did back in Wooden's day. And that means a visitor can still get a sense of what two trainloads of Shelbyville fans saw when they first gawked at the monstrous facility on the night it was dedicated … and, for the record, the night their boys beat the eventual state champs 47-41.

Basketball Bunkers

And you thought only baseball fields had dugouts? Not so in Colcord, Oklahoma, where the home and visitor benches are located in dugouts. Located below the court level, they are situated under the bleachers, a kind of bunker away from the fans. Opposing teams sometimes have a difficult time adjusting to the unique environment and low ceilings. Reminders are painful. "If the coach or players get too excited and jump up, they can get a knot on the head", explains Bill Earp, Colcord's boys basketball coach.

Submitted by Dale Reeder

PANTHERS' PRIDE

"This is basketball country -- land of Rupp Arena, single division high school basketball and legendary coach, Rick Pitino. Like Indiana, high school basketball is king. Augusta is my choice to represent Kentucky hardwoods. The story is best told by Robin Kelsch, a native of Augusta, and their longtime high school basketball coach. His love for his hometown and Panther basketball shines vividly through his written narrative."

Noted author, Walter Rankin, once wrote about Augusta:

"Nestling among a bower of trees on the edge of the Blue Grass Region of Kentucky lays the town of Augusta. It's one of the most beautiful situations on the Ohio, where the river runs in a direct course for several miles, and the sunsets send a riot of color aloft to the gold clouds against the blue of the early evening sky, while the shadows of light and dark silhouette the high Kentucky hills, and as the day closes, a blanket of purple and grey envelopes the low rolling Ohio hills that seem to extend down to the very water's edge of the river's bend, to make the setting and the scene one of the most beautiful in all the world."

Rich with history, beautiful buildings and down home people, Augusta often referred to as Mayberry, offers people a chance to get away from the hustle and bustle of the big city and relax. You can see why I am proud to call Augusta home.

Augusta was part of a Revolutionary War grant given by Virginia to Captain Phillip Buckner and received its charter on October 2, 1797. Since it was incorporated in 1797, it has remained a primary stopping point for tourists and travelers alike. Whether they have come by boat, by train or by car, in some way they have all been a part of Augusta's storied history.

In 1880, only three years after its incorporation, Augusta started running a ferry to take people back and forth to Higginsport, OH. The Augusta Ferry still runs daily and is one of only two still in operation in Ohio. In 1822, the first established Methodist College in the world was opened in Augusta, KY. In 1862 during the Civil War, John Hunt Morgan's raiders burned and looted the city of Augusta. It is documented that Stephen Foster wrote part of Kentucky's state song, "My Old Kentucky Home," while visiting a relative in Augusta, KY.

Augusta High School, Kentucky …Credit: Robin Kelsch

If you love Kentucky High School basketball, do yourself a favor and come to my home town. First stop…..the high school gym, affectionately referred to as the Panthers' Den! When seeing it for the first time many opposing teams look around and quickly compare it to the gym in Hoosiers. The floor is barely long enough to meet the minimum requirements to play on. The gym is so small that it is not uncommon for the referees to have to ask the people on the front row of the bleachers to have to scoot apart so the player inbounding the ball has enough room. On the west end of the gym the wall is less than two feet from the baseline, and on the east end the stage is only six to eight feet away. When you add the fact that the cheerleaders from both teams cheer on that end of the court, it is safe to say that there is not a lot of extra room. I've had people tap me on the shoulder in the middle of a game and stick their head in our huddle. You can't believe the things that can happen in a small compact gym.

A local sports enthusiast turned journalist, Ryan Ernst, wrote an awesome piece describing the gym and the electric atmosphere it provided when our cross-county rival came to Augusta to play us. This rivalry may not pit the best players in the state going at it, but it is definitely one of the most intense rivalries across Kentucky. For years, our small independent school, and Bracken Co., the bigger county school, have battled twice a year for bragging rights that last a lifetime. In his article these are the words he used to describe the Augusta Gym:

"Four rows of unretractable wooden bleachers adorn a balcony on both sides of the court. There's an identical setup on the floor, where first-row spectator's feet come dangerously close to the court. Fans walking from one end of the gym to the other are forced to walk on to the playing surface, often during live action."

Ernst was so moved by his basketball viewing experience on his trip to the Augusta Gym he penned the quote, *"If prep basketball is a religion in the Bluegrass, then the Panthers' Den is its Sistine Chapel."*

Similar gyms were once the standard in Kentucky and as population and the popularity of the game grew, small communities traded in their crackerboxes for newer, bigger facilities. Not Augusta….the school board in 2004 decided to restore the old relic. It is still small, but remains the same as it did 78 years ago.

Some area coaches remember when it was worse. "Augusta was unique because the floor was buckled in a crazy way," said Ken Shields, who coached at now defunct St. Thomas in the 1960s and '70s. It was like 'going uphill and downhill.' It was an interesting place to coach. The first time I coached there, half the shower room was dirt. Our guys would come out of the shower with mud on their legs because the water would hit the floor and spash up and get them dirty."

Augusta basketball has been a part of my life for as long as I can remember. My dad starred for the Panthers in the mid sixties and actually led them to enough regional tournament appearances that they were able to put in the floor that we still play on today. It was also during this time period that they moved from wooden backboards to glass backboards. Growing up, my favorite thing to do was go to Augusta Panther basketball games with my father. I can remember walking into the gym when I was very young and thinking how huge and magnificent the building was. My two dreams at that time were to play basketball for the Augusta Panthers and to be old enough to sit in the balcony with the students and the band and cheer on the Augusta Panthers and Lady Panthers. Until 2005, the balcony was almost completely wide open. The safety railings consisted of two small round beams that went around the balcony with about a four foot gap in between them. It is a miracle that no one ever fell from this balcony. Although in my time I have personally witnessed a couple of people jump off and survive.

Proms, graduations, town meetings, wrestling matches, and yard sales are a few of the events that the Augusta Gym has housed since it was renovated in 1926. It has also served as the local skating rink and the place where many of the people in town come to wait out thunderstorms and tornado warnings. Former Miss America, Heather Renee French, was born and raised in Augusta and has performed many times in the Augusta Gym. Survivor favorite, Rodger Bingham, spoke to the students of Augusta Independent School in the Augusta Gym. The sheer amount of activities that the people of Augusta use the gym for make it the center of life in this small river town, but it is the rich basketball history carved within the walls that make this building come to life.

**George Clooney, Augusta's most famous basketball player
...Credit: Augusta High School Annual**

The gym has seen future national stars such as George Clooney and David Justice play basketball on our floor. Justice, a former MLB All-Star, played for a visiting team in the early 80's. George Clooney, better known as Batman, graduated and played basketball for Augusta in the late 70's. All those shots he drained as Dr. Doug Ross on ER, might have come from countless hours of practicing jump shots in the Augusta Gym. Our gym has also seen games cancelled because of ceiling leaks and a game end in a tie due to electrical failure. Throw in all of the game winning shots, last second free throws and thousands of kids scoring their first points (one of those being yours truly sometime in the early 80's) with parents screaming emphatically, and you can begin to get the feel of why the Augusta Gym means so much to me and to everyone in Augusta.

While attending school at Augusta Independent, I played thousands of games in the gym. After graduating from college, I returned home to teach and coach at the school I call home. Over the past few years, I have realized just what significance the Augusta gym has been on my life. It is my safe haven; it is where I have spent four or five nights a week working, living, and learning about education, about basketball, and most importantly, about life. I have raised my own kids in this gym; it has been their personal playground. They have taught P.E. with me and they have coached many a game with me and I wouldn't want it any other way. I am thankful for the improvements during restoration, but glad it hasn't taken away the atmosphere that existed over the years. As I turn out the gym lights on any given night, rather it be after an Augusta Panther win or a tough defeat, I always take a few minutes to sit and reflect on the many memories that this tiny hardwood has offered to help make me the person I am.

Early Day Basketball in Missouri

In 1906, the first indoor game was contested in Lebanon, not by boys, but girls. It was played in the Opera House above Farrar Drug Store on Commercial Street. The audience was seated on the stage and in and under the gallery. On the day of the game, town fathers moved the theater seats into the lobby, thereby creating space for the girls to play. Up to the 1920's, when gyms were built, most games were played outside, making the Opera House a "one-of-a-kind!"

HOME OF A GHOST

"For some reason old gymnasiums have conjured up the idea that many are haunted. Perhaps it's a figment of imagination. I remember as a youngster, after sneaking into our hometown gym, the security people, after giving us the boot, warned that if we did it again the ghosts would get us. After that, I always thought twice before illegally entering a gym at nighttime. It would be appropriate to tell at least one so-called haunted gym story." The following chapter was taken from "HALLOWED HARDWOODS", written by Brian D. Stucky.

Two precious old gyms in the same block honor the city of Oxford, Kansas. This Sumner County town is known for its old flower mill on the banks of the Arkansas River. One gym is and always has been the gym for Oxford Elementary School. The 1930 crackerbox with a wood floor of twenty-seven feet by fifty-four feet (smaller than a modern day volleyball court) is so tiny that the center jump circle is six feet in diameter and even then touches the free-throw circles. One of the rare floors to still show the old "key-hole" on the lane also has the 12 foot lane, outside of which is only seven additional feet to the sidelines and thus the narrowest court I have seen. The boundary still is four feet away from the wall for a row of chairs, and high balconies surround the gym except for the north stage. But the real gem of this gym is the south entrance. A brick "bay window" type structure houses a ticket booth. Imagine the fans those many years entering by this door to see a grade school game. If you like nostalgia, this will bring a smile to your face.

Oxford Grade School; site of high school gym ...Credit: Author

The other treasure is the old 1928 high school gym, now a middle school. Entering the west door, the first thing seen is the old stage with the old curtain with the letters ORHS (Oxford Rural High School) stitched in the brownish fabric. The balcony wraps around three sides of the gym. Structurally original, only the new tile floor replaced the original tile floor of 36 x 66. Today's middle schoolers use it as a cafeteria until basketball season, when practice begins. Old-timers remember Oxford's power teams of the forties that played against Wichita's Cathedral High (now Kaupun) and frustrated them in their tiny gym.

What adds some colorful stories to this already interesting gym has nothing to do with basketball. The recent book "Haunted Kansas" by Lisa Hefner Heitz, includes a chapter on "Oxford Middle School," meaning the old high school. After Billie, a popular sophomore girl at the school (known as a fun-loving prankster) had been killed in a school bus accident in 1943, strange things began to happen in the building. ... a heavy door would squeak open and then be vigorously slammed shut ... two janitors insisted that the second-floor hallway was always cold, even in the summertime. One janitor snorted in derision that there was no such thing as a ghost, was promptly hit on the nose by a falling light fixture, previously thought to be in good repair.

Legend has it that the ghost hides in a balcony projection room above the lunch room in an area that was originally the gym and auditorium. Traditional legend at the school holds that Billie is always present at the annual Kayette slumber party in the lunchroom/gym. This building, known for numerous stories of muffled voices, pipes banging, creaks and groans of an old building, may not be most famous for the basketball played there, but might be more famous for being home to a ghost.

A WET GAME

Lester Ewing officiated area high school games in Indiana from 1937- 1958. Often he was assigned games in small gyms. "A holiday tournament at Griffin, Indiana sticks in my mind," the Evansville man recalled. "It rained for 24 hours and the roof leaked something awful. They put buckets on the court and every now and then somebody would mop up. Running the court, you better believe, the players kept their eyes on those buckets and I don't mean the ones they shoot at!"

Submitted by Lester Ewing

BEDLAM IN A BANDBOX

"Small gyms are often referred to as a bandbox. I wanted to know why. I also wanted to find a gym that best fits the description of a bandbox. Thanks to Clay Latimer of Denver's ROCKY MOUNTAIN NEWS, I was able to find the best example in Flagler, Colorado."

Bandbox is an English expression whose origin dates back to the 1600's, when a bandbox was a container in which neckbands were stored. Later it extended to equate a hat box. In the early days, a bandbox in the US was an old slang word for a local prison where escape was an easy task. Webster gives several definitions: (1) a light cardboard box, (2) a musical term: a room for a band of musicians. It usually has a roof, but is open on all sides, (3) or a ballroom. All the slang and definitions add up to one simple description: a small confined area. In basketball terminology, it suggests a very small room, perhaps even a cracker box, which tells it's a small floor bounded on all four sides by walls.

To be classified as a bandbox some or all the following ingredients must be in place. They have narrow, shorter-than normal sized courts; some are dimly lit with low ceilings and with slippery playing surfaces. (Don't they throw sawdust or like substances on dance floors, to make them easy to glide across?) Its games attract large crowds or what passes for a large crowd in a small space. Finish off with plenty of heat, a rousing pep band and rowdy hometown fans. You have the picture.

Despite their peculiar charms and endearing flaws, most bandboxes were torn down, boarded up or converted into practice gyms years ago. Some are still alive. A shining example is Flagler, Colorado.

Home of the Flagler Panthers ... Credit: Author

The past is thriving in Flagler, a small farming community on the eastern plains of Colorado, about 50 miles from the Kansas border. The biggest business in town sells farm machinery and the closest, major store is some 45 miles away. Teachers remember when they taught the parents of current students. There's no point in high-school reunions because everyone knows what everyone else is doing anyway. Everything about this quaint, tiny community nestled in this rural countryside suggests serenity. Everything that is, except the local high school on a Friday night during basketball season. When their opponent enters the seemingly friendly confines, everything changes. The end of the evening's activities comes none too soon. Most of the time the visitors want to get out with their lives, let alone a victory. The proof is the win-loss record for the Panthers. In the last five years they've won 90 % of their home games.

The following is taken from Clay Latimer's article: *From Interstate 70, the town appeared to be abandoned on most nights, except for the fluorescent glow of a Loaf 'N Jug. On a weekend night in December, "Everybody's at the game," a service station attendant said. "Go down the road, hang a right and go past the railroad tracks, but good luck with the parking."*

The temperature is 30 degrees and dropping, but several hundred fans have made their way to Flagler High for back-to-back-to-back games with the Burlington boys and girls varsity and junior varsity teams. I questioned whether my wife will be able to sit through four to five hours of small town basketball. We were in for quite a surprise.

The home gym of the Panthers hardly is restricted to basketball. Plays, assemblies, town meetings, the annual bazaar, even funerals take place in the cozy confines of the 53 year-old winter haven.

On game nights, dinner is served in the school cafeteria, but basketball is the social magnet for everyone from grandparents to toddlers. "What else are you going to do on a Friday night?" goes a common refrain.

Manning the scorer's table is the school Superintendent. Sitting a few rows away is a 1960 graduate who hasn't forgotten his first glimpse of the gym. Across the way is Jim Smithburg, the Coach who guided Flagler to three state championships in the 1980's, when the gym sported fan backboards and only one scoreboard. He said that during the State tournament they didn't play until Thursday, but went on Wednesday night to Denver (the Coors Center) to get acclimated… to show them, that hey, the basket is still ten feet high and the free throw line is still 15 feet from the basket….like that scene from HOOSIERS!

Busy wall of banners reflects championship seasons
...Credit: Author

Flagler's court is 10 feet shorter than the standard and there is a full length stage at one end, often the building style in the 1950's.

"It looks like a barn," Flagler Athletic Director and the girls basketball coach said. "The floor has been there for so long there are dead spots. You're dribbling and all of a sudden the ball isn't there."

The gym is so limited in space that the outstretched legs of front-row fans practically extend onto the court. "You're so close you can talk to your friends in the stands," said Kenzie Witt, forward on the girl's team. The coziness hardly ends there. Players share the front with fans, often from a rival school. "If you're sitting on the end of the bench, it gets kind of awkward," senior guard Kendra Rand said.

Not surprisingly, Flagler employs a full-court pressure defense, heightening the claustrophobic atmosphere and breakneck pace. During the boy's varsity game, Flagler senior Lucas Loutzenhiser vaulted onto the stage, dodging a cluster of kids. It was pretty exciting. "We all jumped up there to get him off," said Alex Nestor, a senior on the team.

It's just another Friday night in Flagler… 4 games, 4 wins…. the visiting team descends into a dim, dingy dressing room, preparing for the long ride home. For the local team, it's another night to celebrate… in a bandbox built for memories. What they say if you listen in on conversations around the State within the high school coaching circles is this, "People hate to play in this place… they say it's a cracker box; there is no room; people are screaming at you; and you'll get mugged if you fly into the stands going after a ball." The four hours of non-stop entertainment ended too soon.

Oh, by the way, the Flagler boys won state championships in 1980-81, 1981-82, and 1983-84, so the bandbox wasn't a deterrent.

COME ON, SUPERINTENDENT --- Have a Take!

You don't need a state of the art gym to win a national championship. In 1924, Windsor H.S. in Colorado accomplished it. Their gym resembled a crackerbox, with its cramped low-hanging pipes, preventing long shots. On layups players crashed into concrete walls. Wooden tiles on the floor were so warped and twisted that dribbled basketballs went off in crazy directions.

The coach attempted to raise money to replace the overhead pipes and floor tiles. When he complained to the Superintendent, his response was, "Tell the boys not to dribble and don't shoot long shots." That's a fine way to treat a coach who just won high school's March Madness!

THE OLD BARN

"I spent the 2006 basketball season in Tulsa, home of Oral Roberts University. The women's coach is my son, Jerry Finkbeiner. While there, Jerry learned of my interest in writing Vanishing Hardwoods and recommended I visit Welch High School, widely known around Oklahoma basketball circles as the gym to have the toughest home court. After spending an afternoon with retired coach, Ken Sooter, I was hooked. The Welch gym has a story to tell and I want to be the teller."

You don't just happen upon Welch. The small community of 540 citizens is tucked away in the rolling hills and ranch land of the far northeast corner of Oklahoma. Some say, "It's not at the end of the world, but it sure is close." Here in this tranquil setting, one finds a community and gym that conjures up visions of early day basketball, reminiscent of the movie "Hoosiers."

My first stop was at the home of Kenneth Sooter. At age 80 and retired, Sooter spent his entire career of 37 years coaching kids at Welch schools. After a few introductions, I was escorted into Coach Sooter's den, where the wall is filled with hardware, all speaking to his coaching legacy. *"All of my awards came from my service to students,"* he says, scoffing at all the fancy plaques and trophies. *"Give the credit to those kids and their families."* The coach was too humble to give the facts behind the awards. Knowing he is in several Halls of Fame will defend the crowded wall. Furthermore, his career win-loss record for boy's team is 569-124 and for the girls, 434-126, is a testament.

Welch's Old Barn ... Author

I was there to see the gym. A short walk brought us to the classic building, built in 1950 for a little less than $50,000. I was impressed with its handsome appearance. The hallowed hall has stood the test of time. The students affectionately call it the "old barn." Inside it didn't take long to understand why visiting coaches hated to play here. One opposing coach was heard to say, *"You come to my place and I'll give you 15 points."* Not a bad idea, for over a stretch of 12 years, Welch never lost a home game.

Coach Sooter walked to one end line and pointed to the out-of-bounds that was tight up against the wall. He said, "On standing room only nights, folding chairs are placed against the wall and because there is no room, spectator's feet are in the field of play." He continued by saying, "We then had to go to a restraining line." For modern day basketball fans, a line is painted 3 feet inside the boundary and an opposing player must not invade that space on in-bounds passes. Back to the row of chairs on the baseline…one chair was always removed allowing the in-bound thrower a space against the wall to make the pass.

The placement of the backboards on the end walls furthered hampered visiting teams. *"We saw many players bang into the wall on lay-ups. Our players could adjust, but I often feared visiting players not accustomed to the* wall *might injure themselves. Of course, when they missed, I didn't mind,"* he laughed.

One of the most unusual aspects of the facility was how the substitutes entered the game. This was because the scorer's table is located across the court on a stage, opposite to where the player's sit. A large "X" is painted on the floor outside the field of play. Before a sub could enter the game, the player had to stand on the mark and get the attention of the scorer. To be noticed, the sub would frequently wave frantically as a signal to enter the contest. This illustrates why it's a difficult place to play. One opposing coach had this to say, *"You better be 10-15 points better or you can mark up "L" before you even step on to the floor.*

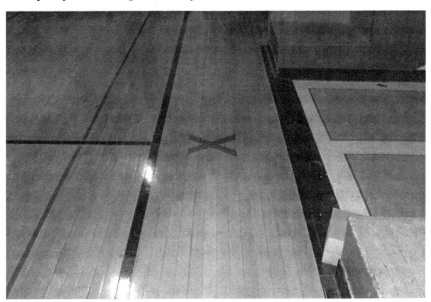

X marks the spot where subs check in ... credit: Author

A celebrity or two have bounced balls on this court. Mickey Mantle, from nearby Commerce, traded in his cleats for a pair of sneakers and competed on this floor. After becoming a Yankee, Mantle brought a few of his old high school teammates to Welch and played a benefit game against some of the local natives, including Coach Sooter. Ralph Terry, another Yankee, who hailed from nearby Chelsea, performed on the court during his High School days. The gym didn't compete with Nashville, but on its tiny stage, it played host to some of America's top country artists, including Johnny Cash and Roy Clark.

The diminutive gym played a role in a controversial issue for Major League Baseball. In the mid-fifties, baseball teams offered bonuses to young players. Paul Richards, manager for the Baltimore Orioles, offered young Bruce Swango, a Welch basketball and baseball player a 36,000 dollar contract to make the jump from high school directly to the major leagues. Bruce, during his senior year averaged 17 strikeouts a game, so the Pros thought he would be a no-miss prospect. Swango had an easy smile and an infectious Oklahoma twang and many qualities necessary to make it in the big-time. But things didn't work out. He was so wild in batting practice, his teammates were reluctant to step into the box and hit. The Orioles abruptly released him after only nine weeks, despite owing him his $36,000. Several similar incidents prompted MLB to forgo the "bonus baby" signings.

Later the circumstances surrounding Swango's signing were revealed. Oriole scouts watched Swango throw inside the Welch gym. His fast ball sounded a lot faster than it was, when the ball popped in the catcher's mitt. The sound would reverberate and echo throughout the gym. Evidently his fast ball impressed the scouts and was signed. For several years Bruce moved about in the minors, never to return to the big time. To his credit, Hugh Alexander, a scout for the Chicago White Sox and a former teammate of Bobby Feller made this comment, "Bruce had the greatest velocity of any pitcher he had seen other than Feller." It was unfortunate that Swango never was able to control his wildness. If he had coaches of today, we could journey to Cooperstown and see his picture hanging on a wall.

Coach Sooter's impressive resume was bolstered by members of his family. Five of them played leading roles in the years when the teams went undefeated. All of them went on to play college ball, including one daughter, Lynn, who played for University of Missouri and is presently, Athletic Director at University of Texas, San Antonio.

After spending a delightful afternoon with Coach Sooter, I learned why he spent his entire career in this tiny Oklahoma hamlet. Paraphrasing some of his comments, "Big city folk can sneer at rural lifestyles and its traditional values all they want to, but I'll take the parents and young people that I've worked with throughout the years any time." Well said and let me add…if this sounds cornball, bring me a second helping!

It took 25 years to pass a bond issue, but the folks around Welch finally decided they needed a new gym, much to the disappointment of the present basketball coach. After all, he'd lose that home court advantage. Somehow, it just won't be the same without the old historic hardwood they have called home for over 50 years. The new gym will have to build its own character and carry out its own legacy, to be earned only through years of games and countless memories to come.

In 2007, the new gym was dedicated and the floor was named, in honor of Welch's number one guy, Coach Kenneth Sooter.

SPLIT the POST

Where did the descriptive phrase "split the post" originate and why do we call the big men in basketball, "post" players? Could it be that in the early days, a post or a wooden beam was built into the construction of the gym? One old gym in Kentucky shows evidence of a post that had been cut off at floor level, near the free throw line. How would you feel defending a player who runs you into an immoveable 6in.x 6in. wooden post? Ouch! Shaq would be a powder puff!

WELCOME TO THE OLD WEST

"Eastern Oregon is a picture of rural America. You can travel hundreds of miles and only see jack rabbits, coyotes and sagebrush. Basketball is the prime sport in the few communities that are sparsely scattered throughout the area that's larger than several New England states combined. The Oregon State Legislature for years has wanted to consolidate the small towns, but hasn't succeeded. I journeyed to one of these communities to find out why they've chosen to remain as one. I found my answer in Monument. Their small gym and the league they play in is like no other in America."

Monument, Spray, Fossil, Antelope, are towns not known outside of Oregon, but their names suggest the type of communities they are. Perhaps this writer should be describing a "shoot-out at O.K. Corral," rather than a "shoot-out on the hardwood." The names suggest sparse communities and as lonely as a train whistle on a far away plain. These are towns where the only winter sounds are the rustling of fallen leaves or the quiet fluttering of snowflakes, where the leisure activities are not supporting symphony concerts, but sitting across from a store's pot belly stove, discussing last night's high school basketball game.

Antelope, population 60, has a mercantile, campground, and a post office. It was originally a stage stop on the Old Dalles to Canyon City Trail. The community languished until 1980 when followers of Bhagwan Rajneesh brought his followers to the area and established a city of 4,000. After five years of controversy, including illegal immigration activities and introducing salmonella organisms into salad bars in neighboring communities, the Bhagwan was deported back to India.

The town of Fossil was literally saved from extinction with the discovery of fossil beds on its school's playground. Scientists and curious fossil hunters came from around the world to search for rich deposits in the community's backyards.

To know what schools were like 90 years ago, journey to Spray. The administrative offices, some grade school classes, and the lunch room are still housed in a stone building, built in 1920. As late as 1950, P.E. was taught on the front yard of the school and football games were played in an alfalfa field across the river. Sometimes Mr. Chapman's cows were chased off the field so the games could be played. The inevitable often happened....players landing in a pile of manure.

Monument's pristine basketball gym ... Credit: Author

Then there is Monument, another example of a small town currently on the endangered list. It's a town where everyone knows everyone. Other places have a Neighborhood Watch; Monument has a Community Watch...... meaning everyone watches out for everyone else. All the kids attend one school, encompassing both elementary and high school grades. For fun, people go fishing, hunting, hiking or just go for a dip in the John

Day River that runs through town. Jeremy Boyers, who has lived all his life in Monument, says "It's a good place to raise a family and a place to teach your kids good morals, how to work hard and how to have fun."

This June morning, Boyers Cash Store in Monument was busy. People come in and out, purchasing newspapers, cigarettes, beer or sodas. Everyone says hello and discusses what they've been up to while buying products from Jerry and Jeremy Boyers, the father and son duo currently running the store.

"We like the lifestyle," said Jerry. "It's pretty laid back and nobody's really in a hurry,"added Jeremy.

A tall, thin man in a white t-shirt stepped up to the counter and chimed in. "It's like living in the '30s and '40s," he said. "Just a nice, relaxed atmosphere." He handed Jerry some cash and walked out the door. They later mentioned his name was Darryl Reinders.

And in his brief appearance in the store, Reinders tied up Monument in a nice, tidy package.

The quaint little community lies about 70 miles southwest of Pendleton as the crow flies. To get there, you drive about 90 miles to Long Creek and 20 miles to Monument. Its population at last count might exceed 100. The town was once a bustling logging community, but with increasing restrictions on logging in local forests, both mills and people disappeared. That happened in the 1980's and today only two loggers remain in town.

I heard about Monument and its unique school system. I ventured up some 200 miles and found myself in a Shangri-La for fishermen, hunters and western fans. To find Monument, one follows the north fork of the John Day, a world-class trout stream. If lucky, one might encounter a cattle herd moving down the highway. Modern day cowboys still move cattle from lower elevations to higher mountain range lands.

The Monument country is a hunting Mecca. Tens of thousands of hunters converge on the area for big-game hunting. The countryside abounds with elk, mule deer and big horn sheep. A few cougar are taken as well as black bear. Coaches of fall sports take a back seat to hunting outings and schools annually have vacations to allow their students to join their parents on hunting expeditions.

I arrived on graduation day. The gym was set up to give diplomas to their three seniors. I remarked about the small graduating class and the principal said, "Yes, but next year's class we'll have only one!"

After a guided tour of Monument's tiny gym, the principal invited me to his office for coffee and a final conversation. I listened to his often-told stories. His secretary, apparently eavesdropping, spoke up and said, "Did you show Mr. Finkbeiner the projection room?"

We returned to the gym. The principal unlocked a trap door in the lobby and carefully dropped a rickety ladder down from the ceiling, enabling the two of us to ascend into a large musty, vacant room above the lobby.

"Follow me and watch your head as we go through the crawl space," cautioned the principal. Opening up into the next room, we came into a cramped, dark area, barely room for two people and some odd, strange mechanisms. When my eyes grew accustomed to the darkness, I saw two large, 35 mm, Hollywood-type projectors. My only reaction was to say, "Wow!" The principal said, "They've been here for ages, probably not used since the World War II years. It appeared if we blew the dust off, threaded the projector, the sprockets would kick in and we would have ourselves an old-time silent Hollywood movie.

The principal was rather vague on the history of the projector, but heard they ran movies during the WW II era. He said, "The gym served the community as a theater and Hollywood first-run movies were shown on weekends." LaVelle Cornwell, who was raised in Monument and attended the school system grade 1 through H.S. graduation, shed more light on the gym as a theater. She said, "In the Fall and Spring, we would have movies in the gym and the entire community was invited. The practice stopped during the end of the 60's. To see a movie at other times, we traveled to John Day to a drive-in theater, 70 miles one way."

A question remained… I noticed a well-manicured football field and a well used gymnasium filled with championship banners. I asked "How in the world do you field athletic teams?" The principal answered, "Dayville, a school with a similar enrollment cooperates with us and add their players to our roster. The boys from Dayville travel the 25 miles to Monument on Monday, Wednesday and Friday for practice, while our girls go to Dayville. The procedure is reversed on Tuesday and Thursday. When the season begins, the home games are evenly distributed between the two schools."

Monument-Dayville varsity teams are a member of the High Desert League. Crane, Harper, Long Valley and Jordan Valley are some of the better-known metropolises that make up the conference. The distances between schools are vast, requiring overnight stays, which makes it a logistic nightmare for coaches. Harper, for example, isn't even located in a town and the nearest hotel is 40 plus miles and usually in the wrong direction for the next day's game. It's easier and less expensive to spend the night on the visiting team's basketball floor.

Housing is not a problem when they journey to Crane. Here they can sleep in the school's dormitory and at no cost. The Crane school district covers 7,500 square miles of desert, sagebrush and ranch lands. At the same time, the area is about the size of Maryland and generates only 100 students. Some who live on isolated ranches travel over 150 miles to attend school, thus, the need for dormitories. Crane also boasts of having the oldest, continuing, residential public school in America.

**Harper High School, Monument's big-time conference rival
...Credit: Author**

The longest trip is to Jordan Valley, Oregon, close to the borders of Idaho and Nevada. It's the most western-like community in the west. The school's mascot is a mustang, which describes the locale. Most of the natives are

Basque cowhands, reputed to be the orneriest, toughest cowboys in all the land. The most popular athletic venues in Jordan Valley are the rodeo arena and the Pelota court, a Spanish version of America handball.

In wintertime, high school basketball takes center stage. The gym literally explodes with enthusiasm for its Mustangs. The cowboys with their ten-gallon hats and manure laced boots can be mighty intimidating to the visiting teams. Opposing teams hope to get out alive and in one piece.

Back home in Monument, the small community and its high school mirrors the other high schools in their conference. LaVelle Cornwell played volleyball all 4 years and has fond memories of her days during the 1970's. She added… "The gym was used for everything from school classes to community gatherings, which included: weddings, funerals, dances, movies, and athletic activities. My parents were married in the gym, both my parent's funerals were held in the gym, and I was married there."

Cornwell added, "During the winter months the gym was used all day and night – the girls practiced volleyball from 6 to 8:00 AM, school was in session from 8:30 to 3:30, with 5, 6, 7, & 8th grade volleyball and basketball teams practicing during their P.E. time. The boy's practiced basketball, and at the same time was cheerleading practice 3:30 – 6:30 P.M. After basketball, the girls had dance team practice or play practice. After-school functions, the town teams (adults) in both volleyball and basketball would practice as Monument played other towns in both sports."

LaVelle continued on, "Throughout the year the gym was used for community dances. We had four to five a year. Cornmeal was thrown on the floor to allow your feet to slide for dancing and protect the floor (questionable due to the grime from outside and the many dancing feet). The stationary bleachers served as a bed for the younger children, as the dance was over at 2 A.M. The dances were split between Monument, Long Creek, Dayville, Spray, Mitchell, and Fossil. A live band played and people from all over the valley attended. It was a great time for young and old alike. Even our school Prom was a community dance with a live band. In 1974 the Prom was moved to the Elks in John Day, Oregon, and was shared with three other high schools."

The Oregon State Board of Education has for several years attempted to legislate Monument, Spray and other smaller school districts to consolidate and combine their school systems. The rationale being, with larger schools the educational programs would be enhanced. Monument has stated emphatically, "they will not support the initiative." The natives understand that when consolidation takes place, the community loses its identity and likewise begins a decline in its cultural activities. Over the years the community fathers have fought tooth and nail to keep its school intact, because they know the school is integral in the community.

The proof that consolidation impacts a small town, one may go to Indiana, the hot bed of high school basketball. Drive down highway 58 to Heltonville and find the elementary school. The old limestone building was once a proud high school, before it was swallowed by consolidation, to create a larger school. Go to the gym. There on a wall is a yellowed photo of the '54 Heltonville basketball team....the team that won the schools only sectional championship. The high school was closed 20 years later and the picture is the only tangible the community of 500 can hang their hat on. As though haunted by Heltonville's story, LaVelle and all her Monument alumni firmly state… "No way the boys in Salem will change our way of life. We like it the way it is. We want future students to have the same fond memories we have of our days at Monument H.S."

The old gym may not be showing Hollywood movies any longer, but one gets the feeling that the gym overlooking the John Day River will not go anywhere, anytime soon. The Monument community will see to that.

Basketball in a Warehouse

Eighty-six years ago in Buhler, Kansas and the occasion was a game between Hill Grade School and Hoffnungsaw Prep. The contest was played in the best available facility, the warehouse of the Buhler flour mill. The brick warehouse still stands today as it was in 1917. The court measured 36 feet by 80 feet, but had a few problems. First, it had eight, nine by nine inch wooden pillars spaced every twelve feet, which divided the floor into thirds. Fortunately, they were heavily padded with gunnysacks and were said to have made ideal screens for the home players. Second, the ceilings were only twelve feet high and thirdly, the basket on the north end was considerably lower than one on the south side. At least the seating was good for the spectators. Twelve flour sacks at one end made for comfortable seating.

Submitted by Brian Stucky

THE TALE OF TWO GYMS

"I heard New Mexico had scores of gyms still standing, but deserted years ago. A former player of mine, Phil Teakell, who resides in Clovis, New Mexico, invited us to his part of the state to look at a few. Believe me, I was in gym heaven seeing so many... just take your pick. Which one to include in the book? I decided on two: Wheatland and Forrest. You won't find them on any map. Each had a short, but rich history -- one that must be recorded."

I heard about a number of old gyms still standing in the middle of nowhere, well, somewhere in Eastern New Mexico. Information indicated they have not seen or heard the bouncing of balls in 65 years.

On a trip to Tulsa I stopped in Clovis to visit with Phil Teakell, a player I coached in the 70's at Pasadena College. Upon hearing that his former coach was researching vintage gyms for a possible book, Phil said, "You came to the right place." The next day we were on our way through New Mexico's vast countryside. In one day we came upon 10 communities or ghost towns, as most of them are no longer on a map. Several had signs to let visitors know the town existed at one time. My interest was piqued by the fact that several of the abandoned communities still had a gym and school buildings standing. Each lonesome structure seemed to ask the questions......What is its story? Why here? What forces caused the demise of the community, the school, the gym? Who played here and where have they gone?

It was fascinating to venture inside the structures and see the backboards still hanging from the end walls. Signs of glory days abounded everywhere. One could visualize a game being played and to even faintly hear the bouncing ball and the cheers erupting from the bleachers. Phil asked, "Coach let's go one on one." To an old basketball coach, it was like being in basketball heaven.

Curiosity sometimes gets the best of us. I decided to abandon the criteria for this book and learn more about some of these unoccupied relics. Perhaps I could find a story. Quay, Taiban, Field, Bellview, McAlister and Ranchvale were a few of the towns we discovered on the trip. Most were founded and settled by Homesteaders. Today, not much remains, perhaps a group of trees, an abandoned store and a foundation or two. There were few signs of former thriving communities. Two of the communities, Wheatland and Forrest, still owned a standing gym. I chose to learn more about them.

All that remains at Wheatland ... Credit: Author

One must journey back to the twenties and learn about the Homestead Act, as it was the primary factor behind the settling of Eastern New

Mexico and their communities. The Act allowed anyone to file for a quarter section of land, (160 acres) free to a farmer who would build a house, dig a well, cultivate the soil and live at the site for at least five years. People came from almost every state in the union to claim free land. They came, settled in, and formed rural communities, often only a few miles apart. The lack of dependable transportation and the poor road conditions prevented commuting more than five to ten miles. Thus, each community created a school to educate its children. Chuck Ferris of Edgewood, who calls himself "the old guy who's been studying New Mexico high school a long time,"said it best: "Where they built a granary, they built a school. That's how a lot of those schools came about."

Entertainment was also necessary in these small towns. After the school was built, a gym was next. During the long cold winters on the high plains, the gyms became the hub for community get-togethers. The most important activity was rooting and supporting the local high school basketball team. Basketball games became a means of showing community spirit, pride and bragging rights. On Friday nights, lights turned off in the neighborhood and in the few businesses. If one needed to see a Doctor or preacher, they would find him at the game.

Wheatland and Forrest document this reality. Wheatland was settled in 1915. Its name refers to the major crop found in the area. In its heyday it had two stores, a post office, and about one hundred residents.

In 1907, Watt Farr, from Missouri, moved to the area with his family and homesteaded his ground. He established a general store and a post office. He named the post office for his son, Forrest. The town never had more than a few hundred residents and a store or two. Most of the people lived on neighboring farms and commuted to school. The last store closed over 12 years ago. Steve Flores said, "Wheatland and Forrest had two of the finest high school facilities in New Mexico." To see the schools and their gyms today will testify to that fact.

Today's GPS system knows nothing about these early two communities. Forest is located 30 miles south of Tucumcari on New Mexico highway 209. Wheatland, or its remaining school and gym, is 15 miles northeast of Forrest on highway 469, 20 miles south of San Juan. On Interstate 40, no signs point to either lost village.

For twenty years the Wheatland Harvesters played impressive basketball. It was rare for the Harvesters to end up with a losing season. Wheatland's 50 students always competed against schools with greater enrollments. They played in 5 district championships, winning 3 of them.

In 1948 the Harvesters were arguably the best team in the state. During this era, there was only one classification. The smallest schools in the state competed in the same division with the largest. Wheatland's record (18-1) in the regular season made them the team to beat at the state. Steve Flores, author of GHOST TOWN BASKETBALL, wrote about the run for the state:

"In the district championship against a larger school, Tucumcari, the Harvesters walked off the floor to protest a call against Jerry Isler, Wheatland's all-star. The refs called the game and Tucumcari was declared the champion. Wheatland qualified for the State tournament as the district runner-up. However, the NMAA was not going to allow Wheatland to participate in the tournament. The team waited in the motel room in Roswell until early in the morning before they got the news that they were allowed to play. Wheatland then drew the #1 ranked Portales Rams in the opening round. Exhausted from the ordeal, Wheatland gave the Rams a run for their money, but fell short in the final quarter. Portales went on to win the Championship. The Harvesters went on to win four games to capture the consolation championship. During the run in the loser bracket, the Harvesters ran up against Albuquerque High, which had an enrollment of 2,000 students, and in one of the major upsets in the history of New Mexico to pull off a win against this much larger school was quite an accomplishment, for a team with only 30 students. Wheatland finished that season with an impressive 24-3 record."

"Let's win this one for all the small schools who never had a chance to be here." This speech was made in the movie HOOSIERS just before the Hickory Huskies played South Bend Central for the Indiana state championship. Forrest is New Mexico's equivalent of the Huskies in the movie. Their high school enrollment never exceeded 100. Usually it was less than 50, yet, not only did Forrest win the state championship in 1931, but also two years later in 1933. The Pirates played basketball for 30 years, during which they made the state tournament 16 times. This was remarkable! Most schools that have played basketball for 80 years or more have not made the state tournament that many times.

During the championship run of 1931, the Pirates had a graduating class of 7, and they defeated Albuquerque with a senior class of 1,000. The next year (1932) Forrest did not score a field goal against Albuquerque in the semi-finals. This was the only time in history that a team failed to score a goal. Perhaps it was a revenge game, for the loss it sustained to Forrest in the 1931 semis.

The story isn't over. Move the calendar forward to 1951, just seven years before the school closed its doors. H.L. Quist, player of note from Albuquerque High School, relates in a book he authored, BULLDOGS FOREVER, a humorous incident that occurred between his school and Forrest.

Forrest, Home of the State Champs ... Credit: Author

"I made the travelling team and our record was 5 wins, 6 losses. We eked out a 2 point win at Tucumcari at the rattlers gym on Friday. Three of us must have been in a celebrating mood. What action we hoped to discover in this sleepy ranching community that rolled up it's sidewalks after 10:00 defied logic, but imagination can be the root of all evil in the minds of teenagers. We discovered trouble. We attempted to sneak back into the hotel after curfew, only to be caught by Coach Heinsohn.

Tom Curley, Dick Trott and I were left off the playing roster the next night at Forrest. Since I was relegated to the role of observer, I made some observations as David was about to smite Goliath.

Forrest, which had to be the town's founder's name because there were very few trees in sight, is a peanut-sized farming community on the plains of northeastern New Mexico. Our big city bus driver had difficulty finding it on the map and drove through the town several times before he realized the city limit signs back to back. There were, as I remember, only seven players on the Forrest team and one of them was probably an eighth grader. He was dwarfed by the cheerleaders.

It was a bitterly cold January day with the wind and dust blowing in our faces as we stepped off the bus dressed in sport coats and ties. Coach Heinsohn's dress code was mandatory no matter the environment. Our attire was out of place in Forrest as tuxedos would be at a "stomp" (western) dance. We quickly made our way into the crackerbox sized gym which would be the platform for our performance in a matter of hours. With the bleachers encroaching onto the gym floor and one of the baskets protruding from a stage more accustomed to student assemblies than an athletic contest, we appeared to be on a court the size of a volleyball court.

'I think we're playing the Lilliputians tonight,' our coach said as he laughed,' you couldn't get two regular-sized teams onto this floor at one time.'

I think the coach thought he had reached the outer limits of the boondocks when he coached at Wagon Mound. Now this. Not a highlight on his coaching resume. He must have sensed that Waterloo awaited his army as he shook his head in disbelief while jabbing his toe on the floor to see if it was hardwood.

'Spider,' Coach called out to Jack, given Jack's lanky build, 'Go with the manager and see if there is a dressing room for us. I wouldn't be surprised if we had to dress in the bus.'

> *What I observed and the team experienced over the game's 32 minutes was unforgettable. The hustle and the scrambling on rebounds and loose balls by an opponent, was too much for the Bulldogs. Let's just leave it at that!"*

Forrest and Wheatland are classic examples of vanishing hardwoods. Journey to these two communities today and find the sad remains of the two schools and their gyms. The two community's downfall mirrors New Mexico's other vanishing towns. Records show 79 fewer high schools today than in the 30's.

Again quoting Steve Flores, from his book, GHOST TOWN BASKETBALL, seemed to answer why and how these communities became ghost towns. *"The economy was tied to ranching, farming, mining and the railroad. In many cases, people moved to New Mexico from the Midwest unaware of dry land farming and ranching available in this new country. They couldn't produce the same crops in New Mexico's harsh winters.*

Many mining communities closed in the 40's and 50's, as our country shifted from coal to natural gas. When the mines closed, the towns died. The railroad also played a major role in the rise and fall of these small towns. Railroads transported people and goods to all parts of the country. A depot stood in almost every little village. It was literally a lifeline. In the 1950's, Interstate highways and the trucking industry began to replace the railroad. Villages dependent on the railroad faded away. Third and fourth generations lost interest in farming and migrated to urban areas to further their careers. When the older generations began dying off, homes were abandoned and the final death knell was planted."

A drive through this countryside reveals a ram- shackled home here and there. The land, once fertile fields of wheat and corn, hosts rusty combines and weed-infested vacant fields. The scars communicate a story of a better time when life was vibrant, rampant, and abundant.

Wheatland and Forrest High Schools had short lives, uncommon, as we think of schools with long histories. Wheatland lasted 21 years and Forrest endured only 9 additional years. In today's way of thinking, only a blip on the radar screen. While their existence is short, their basketball histories were legendary. Their stories set a dynasty standard worthy of envy.

The journey through Eastern New Mexico was bittersweet. I agree with Karen Boeler when she writes, "driving through the back roads of New Mexico, signs of those glory days abound everywhere and offers a fascinating glimpse into the history of high school sports." But, as I ventured inside and saw floors of tangled and splintered boards, graffiti on the walls, invoked a sense of sadness. My spirit lifted as I paused for a moment and said goodbye. It was as if the gyms were saying to me, "We're a testament to a bygone day when basketball flourished. Long may we stand!"

Game Called Because of Rain

During the late 60's Chimacum High school, near Port Townson, Washington, played in an old gym nicknamed the Cow Palace. On one particularly cold night, a cloud formed over the court, because of cold air from a couple broken windows and heat coming from a capacity crowd. The referee in charge had no choice but to suspend play. A fan suggested all the doors be opened to allow more cold air in. After 30 minutes, the cloud lifted and the game resumed.

THE LITTLE TOWN THAT COULD

"I thought I was alone in writing a book on vintage gyms. Not so. While in Tulsa, an ORU player from Kansas gave me a book entitled, "Hallowed Hardwood, Vintage Basketball Gyms of Kansas." I contacted the author, Brian Stucky, who generously suggested a gym or two that would meet the criteria for inclusion in my book. Weskan High School caught my attention and on our trip home to Idaho, we went out of our way to visit this quaint middle-America community. It has a heartwarming story line that will be unique to the book."

Every morning the farmers of Weskan, Kansas meet at the co-op grain elevator to have coffee and discuss current events. These are tough times in Weskan, with the economy and the recent drought plaguing the area. Aside from the economics, the countryside is beautiful and never ending, with the land and sky dwarfing the town.

There isn't much to Weskan, located just a few miles from the Colorado state line. Weskan has no stoplights, four churches, and one paved road. The "road hog" in front is probably a farmer's combine. Connie Okeson, local Weskan native, says "There is a main street, it's just not paved." Locals tell me you have to name at least six surrounding towns to explain to people where you're from.

In times past, one could order a burger at the Weskan Mobile café, but no longer, it's been shut down. To eat at a fine restaurant requires a twelve mile ride to Sharon Springs. There's a Wal-Mart 45 miles away in Goodland, and it's about the same distance to the closest hospital in Tribune.

Since 2000 the talk around the water cooler has been about Todd Okeson who took his basketball skills to the University of Nevada. Todd honed his game in Weskan on the family farm, where corn, sunflower and wheat is grown. He averaged 30 points a game as a 145 lb. high school senior and was named Kansas Division 1-A Player of the Year. Because the division includes only schools with enrollments of 85 or less, Todd gained almost no attention. Todd comes from a long history of Okesons, who played basketball in Weskan. Grandpa Ken, the patriarch of the Okeson clan, toiled in the original gym built in 1920.

Restored gym, now used by the H.S. volleyball team ... Credit: Author

The Weskan community did what other communities should do. The old gym, recently restored, now sparkles like a jewel. The gym has a balcony and wainscoting, a stage, projection booth, and a cast-iron spiral staircase in the corner leading to the balcony. The credit for restoration goes to former basketball coach, Larry Colley.

The gym, not close to today's standard floor length and width, remains as a practice court for Weskan's championship volleyball teams. The fan shaped basketball boards are still in place and a shiny glass board has been installed at mid-court along one side. A keyhole and three point line is painted on the floor, so grade school teams can practice on their half-court game. The tiny gym is busy and to hear voices of youthful athletes running up and down the court is music in one's ear. If one spends enough time around Weskan, one soon learns, if it's not round and doesn't bounce, it doesn't matter.

Aside from the vintage gym, a story must be told. There is more to Weskan's basketball history than the tales of Todd Okeson. Sons and daughters immerse themselves in sports their moms, dads, aunts, uncles and cousins played before them. Basketball is passed down like clothes from generation to generation. Three families boast membership on every championship and great teams since 1927, when the old gym made its debut. The three names include: Cox, Welsh and Okeson.

The family histories and their athletic accomplishments read like a Who's Who in sports. Ken's son, Don played at Fort Hayes State. Another son, Dave played for Gene Keady at Hutchinson Community College. Clint played at Bethel, while Darrel played basketball at Bethany College. The list of grandkids starts with Nick, then Eric who played at Colby Junior College. Wendy upheld the women side of the family, who broke every basketball record at Barton County Community College. She won a scholarship to the University of Missouri, where she continued her All-Star career. Todd, as mentioned earlier, when finished playing at the University of Nevada, played for the ABA franchise at San Jose. He concluded his career by playing with a professional team in Finland.

There is more to the story. I visited Weskan for pictures in the spring of '08. While preparing to leave the gym parking lot, a car drove up and the occupants were Connie Okeson and her daughter. They just returned from the Kansas State Girl's Tournament, where Weskan finished in the runner-up position. The Wolves were led by an Okeson.

John Welsh is the head of the second family, which included Beverly, who starred in volleyball and track at Bethany College. Recently she was inducted into her Alma Mater's Hall of Fame. Now the grandchildren are keeping the tradition going. Jason plays football at McPherson; Stacey basketball at Hutchinson; Mark track at Dodge City; and Angie volleyball at Colby. That generation isn't complete without mentioning Keara, who attended school next door at Sharon Springs and eventually became a top pole-vaulter in college.

Add the Cox family to the mix. Leonard played on Weskan's championship baseball team in 1947. His children, Mike and Kevin played for Fort Hays State, while Tracy participated in football at Pratt, and Tori played for Weskan's volleyball teams during her high school career.

Throughout history, it can be said, a number of Kansas colleges made their living recruiting Weskan players, especially if their last names were Cox, Welsh and Okeson. The community of Weskan challenges any town in America, under the population of 200, to have as many of its athletes go on to college.

Billie Cox, a farmer who also serves as the school's basketball coach, adds to Weskan's uniqueness. He comments," there are 28 male students in grades 9 - 12, and 22 of them are on the basketball teams." Out of those numbers came, Todd, who as one of the farmers at the grain elevator said, "he's as big a deal as we've had around here."

Les Carpenter, columnist for the Seattle Times accurately describes Todd's stature. *"They've been forever underestimating Todd Okeson, just 6 feet and a string of bones. At team hotels he is mistaken for a ball boy. On the court, he looks smaller than some cheerleaders; the armholes of his jersey hang almost to his waist. Even his father, who must have watched hundreds of games, looks at his oldest son with disbelief. But this is a mistake. The minute someone thinks Todd Okeson doesn't belong under the lights, with the ball in his hand, is the moment he is deadliest."*

Just ask Mark Few, basketball coach at Gonzaga. It was March Madness in 2004, U. of Nevada and the Zags were battling for the right to move on to the Sweet-16. The smallest player on the court kept diving from nowhere to grab loose balls, curling around men three times his size, and shooting three pointers while falling to the floor. After picking up the shards that shattered Gonzaga's season, Coach Few could only remember a scrawny kid from the tiny town of Weskan who stopped the Zags from going further in the tournament. Todd had the game of his life, getting 10 points and seven assists with only one turnover in 39 minutes of play.

After the game, Coach Fox of the Wolf Pack smiled as he watched reporters surround Okeson in Seattle's Key Arena and commented, "It's a big day in Weskan, Kansas. They're rioting in the streets and probably overturning a John Deere tractor."

The LITTLE ENGINE THAT COULD is a classic children's story with a moral message for youngsters. That book has been used to teach children the value of optimism. Some critics contend the book is a metaphor for the American Dream.

Weskan gym, Kansas – part of the grade school ... Credit: Author

Over the years the little town of Weskan has experienced hard times. Similar communities throughout the Midwest also have suffered losses. Many have been deserted and have become ghost towns. The Weskan train has a long chain of cars and the pull to succeed has been intense. Dust bowls, droughts, deflated grain prices, and inflated farming costs have caused the train to become overloaded and tired. The road over the hill is steep and long. But a little engine came alongside, saying, "I will be glad to help you if I can!" The little Weskan gym kept her doors open, allowing its young people to play and reach their potential. Weskan graduates went on to the far reaches of the state, country and even the world, to bring honor and pride to this little town. The restoration was worth its weight in gold and stands as a model for other communities who contemplate destruction of their gymnasiums.

Today this community has climbed successfully the hill and is experiencing better days. There is no doubt the guys down at the Co-op will have plenty to talk about in the days and years to come. The Coyotes of Weskan High School will continue their winning ways.

SORRY, COACH, for the Interruption

"The Welch, Oklahoma gym had no public restroom with only the men's and women's locker room having toilet facilities. During one halftime, I was busy putting X's and O's on the chalkboard, when out of the blue, a lady came bounding into our dressing room, took a seat and answered nature's call. I was startled and the girls were closing their eyes not knowing what to do. To further complicate the matter, there was no door shielding the enclosure. What seemed like eternity and several red faces, she jumped up and very methodically said as she departed, 'I'm sorry, I just couldn't hold it.' ... only at a small High School!"

Submitted by Dave Wilbers, coach Arkansas Tech

SMALL TOWN, A TINY GYM, AND A HERO

"Tom Brokaw has authored several books that look back on better days in America… "My Favorite Generations", being one. When I came across a piece he wrote for the NEW YORK TIMES relating to his 'growing up' days in small town Geddes, South Dakota, I immediately went about to secure his permission to add the article to my book, "VANISHING HARDWOODS." He generously agreed and you'll enjoy reading about his playing days as a Geddes High School basketball player and a surprising and inspirational conclusion to the chapter."

When I was 8 years old and living with my family in two large rooms on the second floor of a white frame house in a small South Dakota town, one of my winter diversions was an imaginary basketball game played with a rolled-up sock lofted toward the space between the top of a door frame and the ceiling. Although that was almost 40 years ago I remember the inner voice that guided me:

"We're down to the final seconds of the South Dakota State 'B' basketball championship, everyone, and Brokaw has the ball, his team trailing by a point. The crowd is on its feet. You can't hear yourself think. Ten seconds, Brokaw moves to the top of the key! Five seconds! He gives a little head fake, jumps, shoots! It's GOOD!" The rolled-up sock went in every time. My teammates never failed to carry me off the floor. The little blonde girl who coolly ignored my overtures during second grade alphabet recital by now realized what a fool she had been. It was all I asked in life.

**Geddes High School and Gymnasium
... Credit: Eileen Carda**

Alas, I never did win a state tournament; indeed, in the one state tournament in which I appeared I managed to blow a layup, dribble off my foot and, finally, suffer the ignominy of being benched for the semi-final because our uptight coach caught me in the middle of some off-limits horseplay back at the hotel. That was my junior year. The following year I was much more composed and having repaired my relationship with the coach I was looking forward to a triumphant tournament. Then, disaster! We were upset in the qualifying round by a smaller town led by an aggressive guard named Joe Thorne. He was in my face all night long -- my last chance to fulfill a life's dream gone less than a month after my 18th birthday. There isn't a year I don't recall that loss and the enormous hole it blew in my expectations.

Anyway, the current hit film "Hoosiers" brings all this to mind. As soon as I heard the story line I knew I must see it and persuaded my wife to come along. She had been cheerleading captain at our high school but somehow managed to leave behind whatever attendant basketball emotions that brought with it.

Once the film was under way, we were jointly swept up in the sappy sentimentality played out there in the small gymnasiums on the big screen. Sure, the romance between the coach and the pretty schoolteacher was a groaner. And four minutes into the film who didn't know this rag-tag team would surely become the David of Hoosier high school basketball, slaying a Goliath for the state basketball championship, the Indiana equivalent of the Nobel Peace Prize, an Olympic gold medal and an Oscar all rolled into one?

What impressed me, however, was the attention to detail: the shafts of filtered sunlight illuminating the well-worn wooden floor of the tiny gym; the bare-pipe, peeling-paint look of the basement locker room; the sweaty intensity of the players as they huddled with their coach; their friends, family and neighbors hovering over them in those close quarters; the loyal but boorish behavior of the Main Street businessmen. All the harmonics of small-town Midwestern basketball in the 1950's are there.

"Hoosiers" triggered so many of my own memories. The gymnasium in Geddes, S.D., was also the stage. It was elevated about 4 feet above the seating so if you dived for a loose ball you were in danger of a serious crash landing. It also had a large skylight that leaked after a heavy snow. I remember Sylvan Highrock leading a fast break and sliding from midcourt to the foul line. The referee called him for traveling. Sylvan was a Sioux Indian, the only one on our team, and every year he was an especially welcome presence when we played Marty Mission, an all-Indian school along the Missouri River. He'd calm us as we entered what was for us a foreboding environment: a small dark gymnasium encircled by a balcony.

It was there the Marty rooters would stand and chant as they looked down onto the playing floor, where their team would run up big scores as players with names such as John Two Hearts and Charlie Lone Wolf hit shot after shot. Basketball was a year-round sport at Marty Mission and the players owned a home-court advantage quite unlike any other. We didn't have a chance. The greatest shot I ever saw? It was not in a game. One night a few of us stayed behind in the locker room until the school had been locked up. Then we pushed the bleachers against the far side wall. Chuck Gremmels crawled atop them at a point about midway in the backcourt and launched a two-handed shot toward the far basket, jumping from the bleachers as he released the ball. He didn't see the result, but we did: It went straight in, touching only the bottom of the net with that wonderful small, explosive sound.

Tom Brokaw played basketball on this court, which doubled as a stage for the auditorium ... Credit: Eileen Carda

Basketball is much more than gymnasiums and breathtaking shots, of course. It is also a game of rituals and uniforms. Never have I felt more omnipotent than when I pulled on my matching shorts and jersey, all-white tennis shoes and fleecy warm-ups, tops and bottoms. This was much more than throwing a rolled-up sock against a wall or playing h-o-r-s-e in someone's driveway.

The locker room door would swing open. The band would be playing the school fight song. The crowd would be on its feet, cheering as the cheerleaders called out our names: Whistler, Eide, Soulek, Pokorney, Brokaw. We'd swing into our warm-up routines: layups, outside jumpers, offensive rebounding, now defense, all very serious with barely a flicker of acknowledgement for the crowd, maybe a glancing look at a girlfriend or a potential girlfriend. Then, the game! The unalloyed joy of a victory, well played, no glaring, dumb mistakes, or the weekend long pain of a loss, a loss that brought on hard stares and no consoling words from Main Street merchants.

Over the years I've been fortunate to attend a number of big deals: Presidential summits and inaugurations, White House state dinners, World Series, Super Bowls, Kentucky Derbies, Broadway openings and space launches. I've stood in the Kremlin in Moscow and the Great Hall of the People in Beijing. "Hoosiers" reminded me that those long-ago high school basketball games hold their own special place in the honor roll of my memory.

So does Joe Thorne, that tenacious guard who kept me from the state tournament my senior year. Thorne went on to play football at South Dakota State College and won a commission in the Army R.O.T.C. In Washington last week I looked up his name. It's in those directories they have at the entrance to the Vietnam War Memorial. Lieut. Josef Lloyd Thorne was killed in Vietnam in April 1965, just a month short of his 25th birthday.

A Wooden Building to Play a Little Basketball

The old Folsomville, Indiana gym was nothing but an outbuilding. No bathrooms. No concessions. No nothing. The visiting dressing room was located in an adjacent classroom, which had a pot-bellied stove. The guys on the team had to hold their water for the entire game, and when they got back to the classroom it was a desperate situation. One former player said, "All we knew to do was go in the stove. When they fired it up for school on Monday, it would have been pretty bad."

Submitted by Noble Hunt

HOOSIERS, IT'S NOT

"Upon entering the North River gym, my first observation was that there were only four banners hanging on the wall and they were for winning sportsmanships! For a gym 80 years old, one would think there would be banners denoting championships in basketball and other sports. I wanted to know why."

Brooklyn.... Ebbetts Field, Coney Island and a New York Burrough? No, I don't think so. It is Brooklyn, Washington, end of the road, scarcely on a map, and a community that very few people, even Washingtonians, know about. In the past, it was a home for flower children and at the turn of the century, the site of a rowdy and notorious logging camp. Today, only a historic Tavern and the home school of the North River Mustangs comprise the town. The high school is located where the blacktop ends, a 90-minute roundtrip drive to the nearest post office. If one wishes to buy a loaf of bread, it's 20 miles one way. Some of Brooklyn's students must traverse a winding, narrow road that freezes over in the winter and is hidden in dense fog in the fall and spring. Strangers wishing to locate the smallest school in the Northwest must take 101 South out of Cosmopolis; turn left on Arctic Road; and set the odometer for 18 miles. The visitors will come across a quaint, red brick school house on the left that sits deep in the vast evergreen forests of West Central Washington.

In 2008, I travelled to Brooklyn to take pictures and gather stories to include in VANISHING HARDWOODS. In preparation for the visit, John Barnes, long time North River basketball coach and now in retirement, invited some of his former players to come together. He and I expected a dialogue with the hope some tales would surface, apocryphal or otherwise.

Reunion of players at front entrance ... Credit: Author

The players were eager to share. One remembered a heated contest with bitter rival, Quinault. It seemed a phantom call was made by the referee on a teammate who had a glass eye. Upon removing the eyepiece, he handed it to the ref and said, "Here, Mr. Referee, you need this more than I!"

Much of the discussion centered upon the team's tiny home court. Built eight decades ago, it is 10 feet narrower and 20 feet shorter than a regulation court, barely 60 percent of normal size. The out-of-bounds room at each end is less than the length of a size-11 basketball shoe. A player inbounding the ball can actually have his heel against the end wall and his toe on the out-of-bounds line, an infraction that officials don't penalize because of the tiny nature of the gym.

North River has never been considered as a possible site for a tournament, because the 3-point line hits the sideline some 8 ft. from the end line. On this court there is no such thing as a 3-point shot from the corner. One can understand why visiting teams hate coming to Brooklyn. Recently a player sprained a wrist when fouled from behind on a layup slamming him into the padded wall. Just off in one corner is a door to the concession stand. Last year, a Quinault player dove for the ball and ended up eating popcorn. Unfortunately, he also sprained his ankle.

Several of the old timers remembered incidents that occurred when the gym was overcrowded with fans. There were only four rows of bleachers on one side and a small balcony with no seats, the total seating capacity about 200. With no fire marshall in attendance, the gym often overflowed with some 300-400 spectators. Supporters were routinely thrust onto the floor, interrupting the play and causing the players to tiptoe around the fans. Those close to the action would find players landing in their laps.

The gym was also remembered as having poor ventilation. When the gym was at capacity, school officials opened windows and doors to let fresh air in. Invariably dew formed on the hardwood resulting in a dangerous and slippery floor. The game would be halted until the moisture was wiped up.

An article in the January 21, 1926 "*Abereeen Daily World*" gave the first hint of a group of young boys desiring to compete in high school basketball. The article stated, "A number of high school boys are trying to organize a basketball team here in Brooklyn. Harry Hale, Elmer Arnold,

James Nicolson, and Richard Allen are practicing nightly in the North River pavilion. See you there."

The seed was planted. It is not known if they were able to play any games that first winter, some 80 plus years ago. Their persistence paid off, as records show that in 1927, the North River gymnasium was erected. Today, that same tiny gym is still in use by the girl's and boy's high school teams. It is possible that this may be America's oldest gym still being used by a high school varsity team.

After 82 years, gym is still immaculate …Credit: Author

The genesis of North River High School and its vintage gym can be traced back to a logging camp, at the turn of the century. A.J. Morley came from Saginaw, Michigan to the land of the big timber, to seek business opportunities. A logging company developed and was incorporated in 1918. In 1927 Saginaw moved its operation to Brooklyn which had all the prerequisites for a successful camp: a railroad, a river, and an abundance of timber.

Early day camps generated tall tales, perhaps best illustrated by Paul Bunyan, the giant woodsman and imaginary hero of the great north woods of America. It was said men would sleep 15 to a bed. Different ones would take a branch and carve it in such a manner as to have sharp points. The men would place the branch between them, so that if one got too close they were severely poked.

In truth, the logging camp was a tough industry and serious injuries were suffered almost weekly. Rugged men and tough animals fought the bitter cold and heavy snows to harvest the mighty forest of the west. Families nervously waited for their husbands and fathers to come home.

There was one resource the Brooklyn camp didn't have --- a school for the logger's children. To attract workers, the Saginaw was forced to build a school facility. During its heyday, the camp employed over 500 men. Add to this number, spouses and children for a fair sized community.

The persistence of the five young men and the need for a school bore fruit and a school was born. Unfortunately, history has not been kind to the small school and more so for the gym. There were more downs than ups. North River always was one of the smallest schools in the state. Finding equitable competition for the teams was a challenge every year. Getting to and from the school was an adventurous undertaking. Snow, rain, swollen rivers, mud slides, not to mention flu, scarlet fever, mumps, measles and polio outbreaks were common perils in the early days. These barriers interfered with school attendance, practices, and games.

WW2 came along and caused more problems. Lack of gas and tires and black-outs along the coast caused some schools to drop athletics altogether. Others cut back to the bare bones for the duration of the war. Post-war and into the late sixties, North River experienced some of its best days. Coach John Barnes came to the school's rescue. From 1963 to 1969 his teams, despite the disadvantages, became the dominating team in their league. Though they won their share of conference titles, they still had trouble advancing beyond their region into the state championships.

The one exception was the team of 1966. They entered the state tournament, but lost both games by an average of 38 points. Going against larger schools outside their conference always proved to be too much. Then along came the flower children.

The 1970's saw the Hippie movement settled into the valley. Their attitudes: anti-war, free love, do your own thing, and lack of respect for anyone in authority, resulted in a way of life that was completely foreign to the local culture. They intended to change the world or at least their little place in North River Valley. A dark cloud seemed to hang over the valley. The bad began to influence the good. Drinking and pot became the cool thing. Attitudes, moral values and all things that make a good school went out the window. It wasn't a place where parents wanted their kids to go to school. Many sent their students to Cosmopolis and Aberdeen.

Attendance in the high school dropped into the 20's and at times into the teens. North River high seemed to be on the edge of dying, but through the efforts of a few, weathered the storm. The State classified North River as a remote and necessary school, and consequently were able to secure financial help to stay afloat.

The idea of competitive sports was removed from the school. The trophies and pictures were taken from their place of honor and were put away from public view, as if they were ashamed of what the trophies represented. The traditions and histories of the quaint little school were being destroyed. Bowing to the pressure of the feel good liberal attitudes, the students changed the mascot from Redskins to the Mustangs and the colors from red to blue. The past traditions were completely removed.

The 70's therefore, was a bleak decade for North River's athletics. Basketball on the varsity level was played six of those years. During this time their record was an unbelievable, 0-89! In the 80's and 90's, competition was at the Junior Varsity level, with little success. It wasn't until the 2003-2004 season that both the boys and girls returned to varsity competition. They returned with a vengeance.

In 2002, Coach Les Lande looked at his eighth-grade class and was impressed with their athletic abilities. He figured it was about time for North River to return to varsity competition. He predicted, "In four years we'll compete with anyone."

It wasn't a popular decision in the community. Old timers remembered when North River returned to varsity play in the late 70's. They got clobbered! "I was hated by much of the community," Lande recalls, "I was nearly vilified by lots of people."

The Mustangs' first year at the varsity level (2004-05) didn't help matters. They were beat by everyone and most of the time, by over 20 points. What made things worse, they had only six players and often finished games with four. The following year, interestingly North River lost every game. Would there be a repeat of the 70's?

The eighth graders were now juniors and the basketball program began to turn around. They won a whopping five games and the tiny gym began to burst at the seams. They still had only nine members on the team, which comprised three-quarters of the boys in the high school.

Coach Lande's prediction, back in 2002, came to pass in 2007. After defeating rival Oakville in Districts, it was on to Yakima and the state championships! Success at the state level again eluded the Mustangs. Two games, two losses, the long trip home, and no banner. Getting to the state was an overachievement and North River had nothing to be ashamed of. After 30 plus years of experiencing the agonies of defeat, heads could once again be held high.

The talk around North River these days is not about the lean years or the counter culture that prevailed so many years ago, or about David slaying the Giant, as North River beat larger schools. Rather, the talk is about the kind of kids who now compete and represent North River. There is a reason four sportsmanship banners hang on the wall at North River. An opposing coach says, "They're clean-cut, polite and respectful ... something that's hard to find these days." Jamie Berg, coach at rival Oakville remarks, "They're such wonderful kids, real respectful, they don't talk trash, they just go out and play hard." Opposing coaches as a group arrived at a consensus when they say, "The North River boys have an unrelenting niceness and you expect all nine boys to look and act like the recipients of the sportsmanship trophy."

This behavior is typical in small rural schools. Wendell Berry, a prolific writer and a defender of the moral economy of rural farm life says this, "Rural community life produces good framers who are loyal citizens, hard workers, reliable neighbors, and loving parents to their children, in addition to being stewards of the land." It can't be said better.

Scott Sandsberry of the "*Yakima Herald-Republic*" confirms, "Their town (Brooklyn) no longer exists, but some good things never die."

You make the call

"I'll never forget traveling to Erwin, South Dakota, to play basketball games. The gym also served as the school's study hall, and prior to the game, they had to remove the desks. The baskets were only nine feet high because the ceiling was so low. The out-of-bounds line was half-way up the wall under one basket. If the ball hit below the line, it was in play. If it hit above the line, it was out. Chuck Webbenhurst was their coach and he always gave his opponents the choice of playing the ceiling as in-bounds or out-of-bounds. Webbenhurst always advised us to call it in-bounds, as his teams were very adept at banking shots off the ceiling."

Submitted by Jim Marking

IMPROBABLE HEROES

"How could I not forget Bellfountain High School? I was four years old when my family lived in Shedd, just 15 miles from this small Oregon community. It was in 1937, when the biggest event in the state's basketball history occurred. Some say it was the most incredible "David vs. Goliath" contest in high school basketball annals. I was too young at the time to appreciate the happening, and also sorry that Dad never took me to a Bellfountain game that year. It's taken me 71 years to finally see the gym and I was taken back in time. I'm so thankful that the tiny structure still stands. The best account of that unbelievable season is in a book, entitled THE BELLFOUNTAIN GIANT KILLERS, written superbly by Joe Blakely. Much of the narrative for this chapter has been taken from his book, and I sincerely thank him."

Four miles off old Highway 99W in the southwest corner of Benton County is the intersection that forms Bellfountain, Oregon. Settled in the 1840's on donation land claims, the town was named for the Ohio town of Bellfountain. Near the intersection sits an abandoned, dilapidated storefront with a sign on the window that reads "Gone Fishing." The day I was there, it appeared that all 15 residents took the advice. Out front, two eroding gas pumps stand forlornly. It appears gas hasn't been pumped in decades. Up the hill is a well-kept community church, apparently the only building in town that is still functioning. It appears to be the mainstay in the area, adorned with an age-old, spire-topped steeple. Across the street is what's left of the school. Built in 1908, the school housed twelve grades in five classrooms, two of which were used for the high school. Its gymnasium, located next door, was built about 1913. Bellfountain's families decided their children needed some athletic endeavor other than football and baseball which required more students. Basketball was the answer.

I sauntered into the tiny gym…. my mind shifted into a fantasy world. I listened for sounds emulating from the hardwood…. the squeak of sneakers… the thump, thump, thump of basketballs. I strained to hear the roar of fans and looked for a bevy of cheerleaders leading the home team onto the floor.

I could even see a player decked out in floppy socks, making a no-look pass behind his back. I looked to the far end and caught a glimpse of a player flying through the key, ending with a thunderous dunk that literally shook the rim and backboard. I pause for a moment and ask myself….am I dreaming? Reality sets in. At midcourt, just beyond the sideline sits a rather odd looking, dark black, cylindrical tank-like contraption….something I've never seen before. I look closely…… could it have something to do with heating the gym? It must be…. the tank is encased by a heavy shield, intended to prevent fans and players from serious burns.

Early day source of heat …Credit: Author

I walked under one of the backboards attached to the end wall with unfinished, unpainted, rough 2x4's. It was regulation size, but its construction was unique, as if a local farmer, woodsman, or a student had laid the boards side by side and nailed into place. The sides looked to have been cut by a crude handsaw.

Not much room for spectators. During their championship years, the town of Corvallis brought loads of fans to their game with Bellfountain and I wondered how they could crowd hundreds of fans into this crackerbox? That was confirmed when my attention was directed to the sideline walls where 2x12s were attached to the wall along the entire length of the gym. They were supported by 2x4s approximately every 6 feet and nailed to the floor. It appears the rough cut timbers were not people-friendly, as I'm sure they probably gave off irritating splinters!

Joe R. Blakely, in his book, THE BELLFOUNTAIN GIANT KILLERS, described the court as it appeared in 1913. *"Basketball soon became the game in town, and in the gym's early years the court was illuminated for night games with the headlights of Model T Fords that were pulled into open doors at the end of the building. By the 1930's, however, a gasoline generator supplied the lights, two potbelly stoves furnished the heat, and a small building standing 60 or 70 feet away provided wood-heated showers."*

The year is 1937. The first Cotton Bowl was played on January 1 in Dallas, Texas. Later that spring, the Golden Gate Bridge was opened for traffic in San Francisco. Howard Hughes made headlines, when he flew from Los Angeles to New York in record time, just over 7 hours. And finally, Franklin D. Roosevelt was inaugurated for a second term.

A state basketball tournament was unfolding in Salem, Oregon. In the backwoods town of Bellfountain, a small group of unheralded basketball players was boarding their Franklins and Model T Fords and with their supporters took to the graveled roads toward Salem, not knowing they would become a team of destiny. At the same time, in far-away Texas, spinach farmers were erecting a statue of Popeye… an omen perhaps, as the popular comic character would become a symbolic figure for what it takes to be a winner.

Joe R. Blakely, in his book, takes us on the road to an unlikely championship. *"This was a game that 3,000 screaming fans had waited for. They crammed the balconies and spilled out onto the court at Williamette University in Salem, Oregon, where the semi-final game of the Oregon State School tournament was about to begin."*

"The game pitted Bellfountain against huge Franklin of Portland. If Bellfountain should win, just one game separated them from the first chance in history for a B team (the classification for its smallest high schools) to win the overall state championship."

"From its enrollment of 27 students, Bellfountain fielded a team of just eight boys, making it the smallest team in the tournament in numbers as well as in stature. Essentially, the team relied on its five starters; lose one of them to fouls, injury, or illness, and in most cases the game was lost. In contrast, the opponent, Franklin, could boast of not only a student population of more than 2100 students… almost 80 times that of Bellfountain… but a team of greater size and depth."

"As a result, Bellfountain was the dark horse, the long shot, the underdog, and spectators had admired the team throughout the tournament. It was an admiration aroused, perhaps, from the fact that Bellfountain seemed to dream of doing the impossible, of accomplishing feats beyond its limits, and the team's miraculous victories against overwhelming odds seemed to inspire others with hope for their own personal miracles. But no matter what the reason for the crowd appeal, these eight young men from the back roads of Benton County were proving to be an inspiration in a time when the country was locked in the throes of the Great Depression."

"The referee tossed the ball into the air, and the frantic scuffle began. After a slow and even contest, the Franklin players began to taunt their opponents, using belittling talk to distract Bellfountain, which worked earlier in their game against tournament favorite, Eugene. But when Franklin's players called Harry Wallace an obscene name, the ever calm Harry Wallace responded by dropping in one of his long bombs. In the second half, Franklin scored only

two baskets, and to the approval of the throng of roaring fans, the game ended in a 39-13 Bellfountain victory that put the Giant Killers one win away from an unprecedented championship."

Winning the semi-final was pale compared to their foe in the championship game. They would face another large Portland school, having the advantage of a center standing 4 inches taller than Bellfountain's, Richard Kessler. Remember, in those days a center jump ensued after every basket was made, giving an advantage to Lincoln. All in all, the odds in winning were very slim indeed.

So on Friday, March 19, with the Portland city council announcing plans to experiment with a new gadget called a "parking meter" and *The Portland Oregonian* advertising a five-bedroom house with a basement for $1,950, the Bells felt the tug of destiny as they took the floor against mighty Lincoln.

Back to Blakely's book: *"After winning the center jump, Lincoln found itself pressured everywhere by Bellfountains's defenders. The Railsplitters shot missed and Bellfountain rebounded, their passes coming down the court so fast and sure that their opponent's heads swiveled back and forth in trying to follow the ball as it flashed past them. Sportwriters cameras and their flashbulbs popped as the gym erupted in cheering at Bellfountain's early lead. Bellfountain badgered the Railsplitters at every turn, and at the end of the first quarter held a 9-4 lead."*

"The second quarter was similar to the first with Lincoln controlling the tip and the boards, but missing numerous shots. Meanwhile, Bellfountain, spurred on by the enthusiastic crowd, caused turnovers, passed with pinpoint accuracy, fouled rarely, and scored from the free throw line as well as from the field to take an 18-8 halftime lead."

"Something the opposing coach said at halftime sparked his team to an improved performance in the third quarter. Midway through the period, Lincoln reduced the lead to 22-15. The momentum changed at the beginning of the final stanza and Bellfountain went on to win an improbable victory, 35-21."

"For the game, Bellfountain's impenetrable defense committed just four fouls, forced Lincoln into making only 9 of 64 shots and held star guard Lee Sitton scoreless, while its offense made 10 of 35 shots from the field and 15 of 17 from the line, including Kessler's 9-9 free throw shooting. But statistics aside, the fact was that tiny Bellfountain had done what had been thought to be impossible, and the team's supporters went wild."

"The pandemonium in the gym was deafening, and the cheers of approval ricocheted across the state. Newspaper headlines blazed the news about the small country school that had toppled the largest school." It was indeed David slaying Goliath.

In an editorial headed "Down Went Goliath," the *Oregonian* commented: *"It scarcely seems probable that coincidence arranged for a concentration of basketball talent in a small high school at a Benton County crossroads. Much larger schools have an abundance of equivalent material from which to pick and choose that on a merely physical basis Bellfountain might reasonably have been discouraged at the onset. Nor can one account for such phenomenal behavior by considering that Bellfountain might have an exceptional coach. That much is evident. There must have been, there must be, something else. This something is glowingly undefinable. Sometimes we call it 'class' or 'it,' but never do we quite describe it. It is so difficult to define a spiritual quality."*

**Wooden structure nearly as old as the game itself
...Credit: Author**

There is a bittersweet lesson with this story. Nothing in the world takes away the significance and the team's run to an unbelievable championship season. On the other hand, the most memorable school year would be the last for Bellfountain. In honor of the basketball team's successes, the students put together a yearbook for the first time in the school's history. That yearbook, however, would be both the first and last ever printed. A year later, after its historic championship, Bellfountain consolidated with nearby Monroe High School.

Not much has changed with the gym. The outside appearance looks its age. Inside, the lighting has been improved. A modern scoreboard was added in the fifties. One of the two potbelly stoves remains in place, and according to the pastor of the community church, is still in workable condition. Unlike many early day rural schools, the floor measurements met the minimum requirements of high school gyms. There is adequate room between the end line and walls and good space to make the throw-ins. The community church serves as the caretaker and owner of the school and uses the facilities for ongoing programs.

I stood in awe as I looked at the facility, thinking that here is the home court of a team that made history so many years ago. Memories abound. The gym remains as a testament to a team that accomplished something never to be duplicated. Good for Bellfountain in that they've found uses for the quaint facility that has left the gym nearly intact. In contrast, across the nation countless communities are bemoaning the fact....their important icon, their gym, has been lost forever.

As I departed the gym and bid her farewell..... I thought, basketball, invented by James Naismith, was only 22 years old when you were built. It was okay to be heated by pot belly stoves. At least you graduated from peach baskets to iron rims. Yes, you're crude, rustic and unpolished.... but you're a treasure.

BELIEVE IT OR NOT

Bisbee, Arizona, a city with a storied history, known as the copper mining capital of the world, scene of early-day shootouts, and one of America's most famous western towns. Today you'll find Border Patrol Officers walking the streets. Bisbee is often referred to as a city built on a hill. The high school, built in 1914, had four levels with the gym located on the 4th floor. One of the quirks that resulted from a four- story building on such steep terrain is the well-known fact that every floor had its own ground floor entrance.... an oddity publicized by Ripley's "Believe it or Not." Ninety-five years later, the building is still in use. A plaque on the bottom floor reflects the recognition Ripley gave to this unique structure.

HARDWOOD GLORY, '60s-STYLE

"The following chapter illustrates what we're missing when small towns die out and tiny gyms become abandoned. My thanks to talented writer Ron Vossler who gives us a first-hand report of his high school basketball playing experience at tiny Wishek, North Dakota. Permission has been granted from Ronald J. Vossler, author, and the Germans from Russia Heritage Collection, NDSU Libraries, Fargo, ND 58108-6050, to use the chapter that follows. Enjoy going back in time and re-live experiences that can happen only in rural America."

Each little prairie town boasted its own gymnasium. Those mid-century gymnasiums were the cathedrals of our innocence. Long before consolidation, when television reception bristled with hazy dots, each little prairie town boasted its own gymnasium. It was in those gyms, during each basketball season from junior high until high school graduation, that we enacted our own teen-age dramas, North Dakota-style.

Players and fans alike were caught up in their own Greek drama, prairie-style. There were heroes. There were villains. There was the chanting chorus of the crowd. There was something elemental, close to life.

Our out-of-town bus driver was a farmer named Otto, whom we called "Ottomatic" for the effortless efficiency with which he steered our clunky yellow bus along rural highways in the heart of winter. Eventually, our bus chugged into the neighboring town, which resembled our own hometown only too closely--its two-block main street, consisting of a series of false-fronted businesses, laid out straight as a plumbline between bulky grain elevators and several high-steepled churches.

As we neared the gym for the big game that night (all games were big to us then), we shouted from the back of the bus to celebrate our arrival: "Hey, Ottomatic. Squeal out. Lay some rubber and wake up this sleepy joint."

Wishek High School and Gym ...
Credit: Francis Materi

"Yah, you kits shut up with your big mouths," Ottomatic joked back in his accented Germanic drawl, *"or maybe I leaf you behind after the game and then you haf to grow up here. How wut you like dat?"*

As best we could, on toes frozen into slabs from the bus heater that never worked right, we'd try to swagger like conquering heroes into the neighboring town's gym.

Those evening games were hard-fought battles, for almost all the gyms had built-in home-court advantages. Tiny gyms, ones we called "cracker boxes," were so cramped, we sometimes joked, that the out of-bounds lines were painted on the walls.

One gym had a low ceiling that dropped high, arching shots from the air, like ducks shot mid-flight. Another gym had almost invisible guy wires strung to hold a backboard in place, effectively blocking all shots from one corner, a fact visiting teams learned too late.

There was a rumor that on weekends the smallest gym in our area, in the little town of Zeeland, doubled as a movie theater, dance floor, and even a roller skating rink. It was a fact, however, that if you dived for a loose ball on that floor, you'd end up with slivered knees and a cluster of "raspberries," floor burns that took a month to heal.

My hometown gymnasium in Wishek, hewn from local field stone by Roosevelt-era craftsmen, had huge laminated beams, bolted together to hold up a ceiling as high, I always thought, as a European cathedral's. It also had, we bragged, the best wood floor in the state, presided over with loving care by our janitor, Emil, whose stocky presence was a fixture in our school. Each summer--and one time I helped him -- he sanded, waxed and burnished the floor to its usual immaculate shine. Woe to any student or staff member who dared besmirch that holy surface by walking on it with what Emil called "street shoes."

My hometown gymnasium also had a huge badger, our team mascot, snarling from one end of the gym at all who entered, rendered there in vivid color by our own rural Michelangelo, Jim K., the town sign painter. At the start of each game -- to the fanfare of music and a blinding spotlight that beamed from the darkness -- our players streamed onto the floor from a door which opened between the badger's blood-dripping canines.

The town of Ashley, 30 miles to the south, was Wishek's arch rival -- a rivalry stretching back to the turn of the century, when that town was chosen over Wishek for the county seat. Ashley's home-court advantage was its partisan fans, a deafening mass of humanity who crammed themselves into the Ashley gym whenever our team played there.

Sometimes Ashley fans resorted to German dialect cheers, like this one which I heard while trying to make a free throw during the McIntosh

County basketball tournament in 1965. I don't remember if I made the shot or not, but the cheer always stayed with me: "Blutwurst, Leverwurst, Schwatamaga, Speck, Wishek Hoch Shule, Wek, Wek, Wek." (A loose translation: "Bloodsausage, liver-sausage, headcheese, fat; Wishek High School, away, away, away!")

Thirty miles to the west, in the neighboring town of Linton, players and cheerleaders of St. Anthony's parochial school sported intimidating red uniforms. Even the pom-poms waved by their cheering squads looked like they'd been soaked in blood.

In addition, their rousing school song, "When the Saints Come Marching In," seemed, I thought then, to unfairly enlist the aid of the Deity. (No doubt the reason, I rationalized as a kid, that their team so often beat ours.)

My grandmother, who nursed an Old Country suspiciousness toward those not of our evangelical faith, had taught me only too well. The first time I undressed in the locker room of a neighboring town's Catholic gymnasium, I felt uneasy -- a fact compounded by strange, metallic noises that emanated from beyond the wall which separated our dressing rooms. Everyone on our "C" squad team, seventh and eighth graders, seemed to grown tense. With gaping mouths, we wondered what secret weapon those Catholics might turn against us on the basketball floor.

We learned later that those metallic sounds came from a farm grease gun, as the Catholic players pumped axle grease into their sweat socks to help prevent blisters--a procedure our team eventually adopted.

Gymnasium bleachers were crowded for basketball games with spectators in one town resembling those in all the other towns: squat, solid people, with weather-beaten faces -- the men as bandy-legged and hawk-nosed as the women were broad-beamed. They were the children and grandchildren of German-Russian immigrants, an ethnic group which settled south central area of North Dakota at the turn of the century, an area some jokingly called "behind the Sauerkraut Curtain."

Weaned on hard farm labor, fans watched their children and grandchildren apply that same work ethic on the basketball court. It seemed like all of the players shared the same never-say-die attitude, diving and scrabbling for every advantage, any loose ball.

For the most part, players on teams from our area of the state resembled each other physically, too: In stature under six feet, stoicism pressed into well-scrubbed features, Brilliantine combed into their hair. In fact, it didn't matter if we played in Zeeland or Ashley, in Linton or Streeter. On each team suited up against me, I was sure to find, reassembled in the guise of an opposing player, some version of my own features.

Truth was, on most teams I had cousins, second cousins, or other relatives, by blood or marriage or both -- that far-flung familial network of Germans from Russia. It was our shared kinship, I told myself then that enabled those other players, so often better than I was, to anticipate which way I'd cut, which way I'd dribble.

Our players were mostly "Schtetlers," town kids, who were spoiled and soft from easy town living. At least that's what my own uncle and other farmers sometimes claimed. No doubt there was some truth to that attitude. I know I disliked rough basketball, what we called "plow ball," a kind of playing we blamed on farmers, when elbows and knees were used to raise lumps and charley horses.

Even in victory, we suffered against teams that played "plow ball." Once, our "B" team beat a neighboring town's "B" team by the score of 65-3, and the overmatched team managed to score only a single basket and a single free throw. Successful by the scoreboard but defeated by the bustling physical mass of "those farmers," after the game we could only limp meekly into our locker room, deflated.

Rounded beams, rollaway bleachers, and fan-shaped boards are a good representative of that era …Credit: Francis Materi

Whenever our team played on those winter gymnasium evenings, there were always several preliminary games. Junior high and "B" squad players skittered up and down the floor like wild rabbits. Some young players, wearing hand-me-down, oversized uniforms which hung from their bony frames, resembled starving prison camp victims. To make loose Jersey tops fit better, other players wadded white ankle tape around the upper straps, so that the final result resembled the bulky shoulder epaulets of some banana republic dictator.

But it was the "A" squad game that everyone awaited. The gym filled to capacity. Bleachers were lined with people, elbow to elbow. There was a keen sense of anticipation. Teens flirted around the water fountain. Boys ran wet combs through their hair. Grade-school kids scuttled themselves breathless under the bleachers. They poked their heads up like gophers to see if the game had started; they pulled on people's legs then ran away. Future Farmers of America boys strolled the sidelines in blue jackets, sold bags full of popcorn to finance their annual trip to the state convention.

Finally, over the public address system, starting teams were announced. The frenzy of action began. Megaphones boomed. Tennis shoes squeaked.

Players gleamed with sweat. The basketball thumped and whined sweetly on the polished floor. It swished through the net, it squirted loose into the crowd, then caromed off the rim. Fans rode waves of elation and disappointment. Referees clamped whistles between their teeth. With each basket, cheerleaders scurried onto the floor, arching their backs and scissoring their legs in athletic cheers.

Players and fans alike were caught up in their own Greek drama, prairie-style. There were heroes. There were villains. There was the chanting chorus of the crowd. There was something elemental, close to life.

Then, before we knew it, the final buzzer blew. The game ended. What happened, we wondered? Where did the time go? Players disappeared behind dressing room doors. The gymnasium cleared, spectators filed out the exits, their steamy breath rising into the cold air of the winter's night.

With wide brooms, janitors swept the floor, gathering popcorn bags, pop cups and colored strands shaken loose from the pom-poms. The bleachers emptied, except for some junior high and "B" team players, waiting for the "A" team to dress.

With their scarves tossed carelessly around their parka necks like chivalrous World War I airmen after an airborne contest, the young players -- I was one of them once -- clustered on the bleachers, speaking in quiet tones to comrades-in-arms about the triumphs and disappointments of the evening's game.

They bragged about what they'd done in the game that night and about what they might do in next week's game. How in later seasons, they'd become the best players on the "A" team when the gymnasium floor, the game, the world, or the corner of it they knew, would belong to them fully.

So they waited, clutching to their parkas, make-shift duffel bags, soggy Red Owl paper bags in which they toted sweat-soaked uniforms, damp towels -- waited there for the long cold bus ride over the frozen prairie, with all their dreams of hardwood glory to keep them warm on their way back to their hometown.

What is an Appanoose?

What the heck is an Appanoose? Or where is it located? You're wasting your time looking, for it no longer exists. Yet from 1919 – 1962, it was a rural community and high school located in central Kansas.

In its early days, the gym's score clock was located in the southwest corner of the gym. A skinny grade school lad was recruited to shinny along the wall on a four – inch beam, over the goal supports in order to keep score. When extra number plates fell to the floor, the game had to be stopped.

In 1950, Appanoose and Rantoul were hooked up in an intense rivalry game and just as the horn sounded with the game tied, a Rantoul shot rimmed around and came to a rest on the flange connecting the rim to the backboard. With only one referee to decide the matter, the Rantoul coach sat down in the center of the floor until the Ref decided what to do. He gave the Rantoul players a chance to tip the ball in, if they could reach it. None of them could, so the game ended in a tie.

Submitted by Brian Stucky

TERRY TEAGLE'S LANDMARK

"A basketball enthusiast from Texas, with a fascination for old high school gyms constructed a web site: dean@texasgyms.net, that lists and pictures vintage gyms throughout Texas. His favorite was located in Broaddus. In reviewing the site and seeing pictures of the gym's interior, I noticed the name, Terry Teagle scratched out on one wall. Knowing Teagle was an outstanding NBA player prompted me to find his relationship with Broaddus High School. The result was an intriguing storyline."

Broaddus, Texas, population 89, is a farming hamlet on the Louisana border. It's located near the metropolises of Nacogdoches and Lufkin and gateway to Lake Sam Rayburn, one of the most popular recreation areas in East Texas. The chamber of commerce advertises it as, "A must stop for vacationers and fishermen." Founded in 1904 as a station stop to take on water, the Southwest Railroad became a major transportation route throughout the area and also an important thoroughfare for shipment of lumber from nearby Angelina National Forest. Broaddus became an important hub for the railroad and lumber industry as mills sprouted up throughout the region. During these years, Broaddus's population reached several thousand, but as the lumber production declined in the fifties, the railroad disbanded its lines into Broaddus, prompting people to move on to better opportunities. Hand-poured concrete foundations of the once popular sawmills remain as a testimony to the aspirations and dreams of early century timber barons.

The most notorious persons ever to set foot in Broaddus, were the infamous couple, Bonnie and Clyde. They had relatives who lived near Broaddus and would often spend several days visiting family. A local member of the community, George Lary recalls, "On one visit Clyde was having trouble starting his car, so he would park on the hill side leading up to the school. When the motor wouldn't turn over, he would merely give it a push and away they would go." At another time, Clyde stopped at Ben and Jane's service station to fill up their gas tank. Whether they were on one of their bank robbery sprees or just passing through is not known. What is known, they paid their gas bill with a twenty dollar bill and the surprised station attendant hadn't seen that much cash in a long time and was unable to make change. Knowing Clyde's past history, he could have sped off and not paid the bill. With a Robin Hood syndrome of robbing from the rich and giving to the poor, Clyde merely said, "Keep the change and have a good day." Months later, Bonnie and Clyde were killed in a hail of bullets by law enforcement officers, just outside Shreveport, Louisiana. Today, not much left of the station. The years have taken a toll.

In a struggle to not become a statistic or ghost town, the Broaddus schools became the mainstay of the community. The school understood its importance in the community and the place the gym has in providing a relationship between town and gown.

In 1951 the Angelina Forest Service donated logs from its National Park to the tiny school to construct a gym. Even the local sawmill got into the act, as they took the logs and formed lumber into useable planks, keeping the larger boards for its use and donating the smaller to the building project. Today 50 plus years later, the inch and a quarter wide board's glistening finish testifies to its sturdiness in providing a home court for so many players and fans. Its unique history, longevity and importance to the community, justifies it to be labeled, a 'Landmark.'

Terry Teagle's hangout …Credit: dean@texasgyms.net

When using the word 'landmark', several examples come to mind: The Statue of Liberty, the Coliseum in Rome, the Empire State building and the Grand Canyon. They're popular, historical and important, so most everyone can identify where they are located. Landmarks can also be aids in giving directions, as in, "When you go south on Wilshire boulevard, take the next left after passing the restaurant on your left, with the huge chicken perched on the roof. You can't miss it!"

In Broaddus, Texas, the landmark, although not in the same class as those mentioned above, is the vintage high school gym. To a former high school student, it's a landmark that played a key role in shaping his life. It's a landmark that gave him lifelong relationships. It's a landmark that enabled him to earn a college degree and a landmark that prepared him for a successful career. He'll tell you right up front, "Don't take away my Landmark!"

Terry Teagle led Broaddus to the state tournament in an unprecedented four consecutive years, winning the title in 1976 and 1977. He was named to the 1-A All-Tourney team and to the Texas All-State team all four years, unmatched in history by any school boy athlete. "In my freshman year, when I made All-State, I was only 14 years old," Teagle says. "I was considered the youngest player ever to be recognized as a Texas All-Star.

Marion Neill, his high school coach said, "Terry was by far the best player I've ever coached, and as fine a natural phenomenon on the basketball court as the state of Texas ever saw!" At 6'4", he was seldom out jumped, even by players 4" to 6" taller. College coaches such as Eddie Sutton, then of Arkansas and Guy Lewis of Houston turned up in Broaddus to watch Terry play and would often ask Coach Neill, how high can Terry Jump? The coach's pat answer would be, "I don't know and I don't care as long as he can out jump his opponents and gather 10 rebounds a game!"

When Terry was a junior, the NBA originated the dunking contest at its annual All-Star weekend. Soon the event became the rage and kids all over America began mimicing the Pros, especially Dr. J. It was Irving who first attempted the classic dunk leaving the floor from the free throw line. At a Broaddus practice, Terry's teammates challenged him to duplicate Irving's historical dunk. Terry, a quiet, humble, reserved kind of guy, at first hesitated, but after a continual barrage of insults gave it a try. He took

3 dribbles, picked the ball up at the charity stripe, and soaring through space, he ended up, not with a one hand dunk, but with two! It was during his NBA career that his extraordinary leaping ability impressed the basketball world. Players around the NBA said, "The best jumper in the league was not Michael nor Dr. J, but Terry Teagle!"

A sportswriter from Beaumont, Texas, told Coach Neill about a time when he interviewed Terry early in his professional career. Teagle told him, "My Pro coaches gave me nothing new.... all they diagrammed or said, I already heard back in my playing days at Broaddus." A tribute to the small school's coaching staff.

Terry Teagle returns to his landmark ... Credit: Author

The win-loss record during Terry's junior and senior years was an astounding 71 wins and only 2 losses. During that time, many opposing teams attempted to use the stall tactic, in hopes of keeping the ball away from Terry. On one occasion Central High School held the ball for four minutes of the first quarter, but with the score 6-4, they lost their patience and Broaddus went on to score 100 points. Terry averaged 29.5 points per game his senior year. He once scored 50 and could have scored more, but the coach pulled him out early, so as not to embarrass the opponents. Of all the players on the great Broaddus teams, only Teagle went on to college. Several could have, but they refused to venture out.

Upon high school graduation, Teagle became one of State's most sought after basketball players. Baylor eventually won out and Teagle made the short trip to Waco to begin a new passage in his life. In four years, he became Baylor's all-time scoring leader and was named to the Southwest Conference first team three years running.

The Baylor 6'5" shooting guard was the No.1 pick of the Houston Rockets in the '82 draft and started 44 games as a rookie. In '84, he moved on to the Detroit Pistons, then to Golden State for 1986-90, the Lakers from 1990-92, returned to the Rockets in 1993, after which he retired. In eleven seasons he scored 7,982 points and a combined average of 11.1 points per game. While with the Lakers during the 1990-91 season, Teagle made the shot on which teammate Magic Johnson claimed the all-time assist record. In 1981, Terry was elected to the Texas basketball hall of fame. Very few Texas schoolboys have come close to Terry's accomplishments.

"I've played in all the major university arenas in America," said Terry. "During my NBA career, I played in the Boston Garden, Madison Square Garden and the Fabulous Forum, but nothing compares to playing basketball on Friday nights in the old Broaddus high school gym. Fans jammed our tiny gym where students would reach out and touch players racing by. I can remember tournament fever that propelled us to win two State Championships. It doesn't get any better than that."

Coach John Wooden once remarked, "I'm a Hoosier at heart, but the Bruins are in my blood." Terry would say, "I'm a Texan at heart, but Broaddus High School is in my blood." He goes on to say, "I owe my success in the NBA to Coach Neill, my teammates, and to a small gym in a small community in Eastern Texas."

The town fathers will make sure the gym remains a landmark on one of the few corner blocks in Broaddus. The wooden structure with its donated floor should stand the test of time. On any given day, visitors are welcome to pass through its doors to catch a glimpse of the storied basketball court. The hardwood saw its share of wins, thanks to a legendary coach and to a youngster who later gained fame in the NBA. Lest the future visitors forget his name, a sign still appears on the wall and over the basket that reads, "This backboard and gym belongs to Terry Teagle!"

During Teagle's professional NBA career, it was often noted that Terry came from the smallest high school of any player, before or since. Not an enviable statement, but don't tell that to Terry. He'd be the first to acknowledge, "I'm proud of that fact. I will never forget where I came from." The Landmark will always be there as a reminder.

Just Listen, Boys

In 1950, high school games in Spokane, Washington were played at the old Armory. At halftime, teams went to the same room that was divided by cork bulletin boards.

The West Valley coach was the emotional Jud Heathcote, who later won the NCAA title at Michigan State that featured Magic Johnson. Lewis and Clark was coached by "Squinty" Hunter, a quieter man who eventually won three State Championships.

A member of the Lewis and Clark team remembers going into the locker room at halftime of this important game and hearing Hunter say, "We'll sit here and listen to Coach Heathcote." When it was time for the second half, Hunter turned to his team and said, "Go out there boys. You know what to do." Lewis and Clark won the game.

A CHANGING LANDSCAPE ON THE HI-LINE

"Montana, the "Big Sky" country, ranks third behind Alaska and Texas in size, but ranks 46th in population. 60% of Montana is prairie. Could it be the writer of "Home on the Range" was from Montana? Montana has 500 schools with less than 150 students! It has been said, "Small communities, plus severe winters, equal Basketball hysteria." Joplin, Montana presents a sad-faced portrait of closing schools and disappearing gymnasiums. The following is about one teacher's account of her school's closing."

Montana is "Big Sky" country. The cities are small and the spaces are large. Admiring the expanse of the sky might not be possible amid the skyscrapers of New York, but when city folk visit Montana, they soon understand what "Big Sky' is all about. One easterner who first visited the state, remarked, "I topped off the gas tank in each town for fear I wouldn't make it to the next town. There just seems to be a whole lotta country between cities." The prairie seems to go on for miles and miles and miles. Facts bear out the expansiveness: 46 out of Montana's 56 counties are considered "frontier counties", averaging a population of 6 or fewer people per square mile.

The Montana Hi-Line region is one of the more fascinating sections of Montana. This area symbolizes what Montana is all about – rolling prairie, endless fields of wheat, large herds of cattle, towering mountains in the distance and remoteness – all tucked under the beautiful "Big Sky."

"Montana Hi-Line" refers to the northern part of Montana adjacent to US Highway 2, more or less the 100 miles of Montana south of the Canadian border. The full Hi-Line in Montana stretches from the North Dakota to the Idaho border, for a distance of more than 650 miles. A trip across the Hi-Line is a long one. However, when residents talk about the 'Hi-Line,' they generally mean the part of Montana on US Highway 2 between the North Dakota border on the east side and the Rocky Mountain Front on the west side. The section of Montana tells the story of school consolidation and the impact upon rural schools and gymnasiums.

The map cites 35 communities on this stretch of Highway 2 with a population of 150 residents or less. Also, many more unincorporated hamlets are located on the same stretch of the road. Wander off the road just a few miles north and south of the east-west corridor and the number of small places doubles.

A trip down the H-Line looks no different now than it did 40 or more years ago. Unlike other areas of the state, that have either been heavily developed or over-run by tourists or converted into sprawling sub-divisions, the Hi-Line region has been essentially forgotten.

Several reasons account for the region's declining population. The dust bowl and drought conditions of the mid-west reached this far north, leaving a profound effect. The consolidation of farms and the miracle of agricultural productivity, combined to influence the demographics of the region. Towns sprouted up in the early 1900's, to provide schools, goods, and services to the farms. Later, when reverse economics came into play, the towns struggled to maintain population. In addition, the vast plains tie a diversified mix of coal, oil, gas, as well as agriculture, making it susceptible to swings of fortune from year to year.

A trip on Highway 2, reveals half-empty downtowns, abandoned stores, closed-down grain elevators, and vacant homes in disrepair. The most sorrowful sights are the boarded-up windows on schools and gyms. In the last decade, the number of Class C Montana schools (smallest) plummeted from 130 to 91. Some schools are hardly old enough to have more than two or three family generations to pass through its doors. It's a shame that alumni will not celebrate class reunions in years to come.

School consolidation may be found along the corridor. Joplin and Iverness have joined with Chester. Farther east, the communities of Kremlin, Gilford, Hingham and Rudyard have merged and are now under the banner of North Star. To the South, Dutton and Brady is now Dutton-Brady and asking Power High School to join and make it a threesome.

Unfortunately, the Joplin gym is no longer in use ...Kim Skornogoski

Mary Kay Rambo, now a teacher in Chester's Home Economics classroom, can't help to cry. She formerly taught in neighboring Joplin. For fourteen years Ms. Rambo was surrounded by shining sinks, new cupboards and countertops. The school is now empty except for a scurrying mouse or two, and a few tumbleweeds that have blown through broken windows. All this happened since Chester, Joplin and Iverness merged in 2005. Lockers once lining the now-dark hallways have been ripped out and sold. Sneakers haven't scuffed the glossy gym floor that Hi-Liners are still paying for. Rambo said, "It was a wonderful place to work. It was really, really hard to see it go. We were a big happy family, where the community supported the school and the school supported the community."

In 2008, the consolidation is still referred to as a 'bitter pill. Superintendent Glen Johnson sums it up best, "When you start talking about closing a town's school, it's almost like a death sentence for that town." There's no better example of vanishing hardwoods than along the Hi-Line. The consolidation of Chester-Iverness-Joplin meant closing two schools. A community member bought the Iverness School, hoping to turn it into a community center. It's now empty and unused. Joplin's school was sold for parts. Other Montana schools purchased the basketball hoops, lockers, cabinets, bleachers and library books. Desks, pianos, couches and projectors are stockpiled in the gym. No one knows what will happen to the gym. Natives fear the gym will die a slow death, never again to see youngsters run up and down its hardwood.

Kim Skornogoski in her article, "*A Delicate Merger: Consolidation schools face tough transition,*" speaks to the consequences of school mergers. She quotes the Dutton/Brady Superintendent, "The students had the easiest transition. They adapt pretty easy. It's the parents and the grandparents who remember the good 'ole days that have trouble adjusting. Rather than watch their grandchildren wear the uniform of their former rivals, some refuse to watch athletics at the new school."

Furthermore, merging schools also results in identities and traditions falling by the wayside. Before losing school traditions, new ways of doing things must be established. Skornogoski noted, "A new school needs new uniforms, school colors and a mascot. Trophy cases should be set up in the consolidated school to reflect each of the old school's history and to make sure a record of past championships are not lost."

Consolidation creates dilemmas, for example, which of the schools close and which remain open? One can realize the "hot potato" issues that arise between residents of communities undergoing plans for consolidation. Lest the reader gets an opinion that consolidation isn't the answer, the merge process offers advantages. Increased funding, broader curriculum, more teachers, and the offering of a more diverse menu of extracurricular activities, are all positives within consolidation.

Basketball offers a key motivation to keep and allow gyms to host a vibrant actvity on Friday nights. The heart and soul of the game cannot be denied. The passion of its participants in representing their home towns is a tremendous force to be reckoned with. Basketball gives a reason to resist.

A recent documentary film produced by Jason Lubke, entitled, "CLASS C BASKETBALL: IDENTITY AND LOSS IN RURAL AMERICA," details the lives of a handful of players from small Class C schools in Montana. In her critique of the film, Kisha Lewellyn Schlegel, from New-West.net, commented, "As we followed these players in their quest for the state championships, we learned that basketball is more than a sport for them. It is not just a part of their identity; it is a part of their town's identity." In other words, the players in their quest were fighting to keep their hometown on the map. It was a chance to bring home something worth celebrating. The players expressed sadness as they talked about their home towns. They realized their schools were dying and they knew there was a chance they would not be able to continue living in the towns where they grew up. The girls were more concerned about the loss of the family farms than wins and losses. A heart-stopping message came from the mouth of one player, daughter of a grocer, who cried as she talked about the decline of her town. She told about her parents, whom she adores, and their grocery store which is about to go under.

Lubke, himself a product of a small Montana school, comments, "Basketball in small towns across America, and not just Montana, are struggling to keep their doors open. Basketball gives them something to rally around, something to give them hope." Phil Jackson, the Laker Coach, who grew up in Montana, echoes Jason, "The tenuous spirits in these tiny towns are bolstered by just a few staple institutions and basketball is one of them. The gym is a warm place everyone can go to that isn't a church or bar."

Rudyard gym now in disuse ...Credit: Paul Overly

During the third week in March, eight of Montana's smallest towns are empty. Lights go out, stores close and no one is left to read the message on the theater's marquee…., "See you at State!" Whether the tournament is across state or county, the town's faithful will be in attendance. At the girls games, the boys dress in girls cheerleader uniforms, and in the boys tournament, the town fathers dye their hair in school colors. Winning is important, but to have your home town participating in the state finals engages the whole community.

The game of basketball gives the kids identity and activities. It is the one thing that keeps them sane when their world is flying apart and when their hopes are being sold at the many auctions of deporting people and businesses. Lubke is quoted again, saying "Once the school goes, everything else follows in short order. Keeping the school alive and keeping the team alive is how they keep the town, really. Communities live and die through these kids."

Consolidation might be the answer for some, but with others, places like Hinsdale, Scobey, Nashua, and Dodson, the hope to stay alive rests with their youth. In yet another year, eight teams representing eight small communities will again trek across the wide Montana plains to a common tournament site, vying for the right to be the Champs of Class 'C' basketball and each attempting to bring hope and prestige to the little guy. Hope does spring eternal.

A glimmer of hope appears on the horizon. Kornogoski writes, "Many residents in northcentral Montana's small towns are hoping the agricultural economy will rebound. In the coming years, farmers who chose to take land out of production (as part of the federal Conservation Reserve Program) might be tempted to get back in the business.

A reviewer of the film, "Class C basketball," commented, "The film brought to the forefront the plight of the rural community to not just thrive, but to simply thrive. Rural communities are where the true moral values are and where work ethics and strengths originated. When we lose that base, then we lose that which has made our country the envy of the world." Couldn't be said better!

More consolidation? Maybe, but don't tell that to the remaining communities on the Hi-Line. Most stand ready to fight the closing of their schools. They don't wish to become another statistic.

Only three problems with this Gym

1. *You can't shoot three pointers from the corners of the Paint Rock, Texas gym. There's simply not enough room between the three-point line and the out of bounds to even stand.*

2. *Players lament the inability to throw a baseball-style long pass when inbounding the ball, because there's not enough room to cock the arm back before hitting the wall.*

3. *The three-point line is so close to the half-court line, it's hard to not get into the back-court.*

Other than the above, you can play a pretty good game in Paint Rock.

Jeff Wick, Standard-Times

BEARDEN'S BEARS DEN IS MIGHTY COZY

"As I criss-crossed the western states in the pursuit to find the gyms for inclusion in VANISHING HARDWOODS, my favorite gym of them all was located in tiny Bearden, Oklahoma. What a charming, unique and historical relic. If you ever find yourself on Interstate 40 in central Oklahoma, take the Holdenvill-Briston exit, go south for just 6 miles and you'll find the gym nestled among a stand of sturdy oaks. Go inside, find the Superintendent who will happily take you on a nostalgic tour. You'll be glad you did. A retired Oklahoma high school administrator, Dale Reeder, wrote the piece for coachesaid.com. I had to include the story in VANISHING HARDWOODS."

Bearden School is located smack-dab between Shawnee and Henryetta Oklahoma, in southwest Okfuskee County, just a few miles south of Interstate 40. The Bears lost their high school years ago, but its historic gym remains and is used by the younger grades. "We have a stage at one end of the court and a dead end on the other," explains Superintendent Leon McVeigh, referring to the unusual short length of the gym's playing field. "Our ceiling is very low and only about 18-feet high," adds McVeigh. "When the ball hits it, it is ruled out of bounds." I was told this frequently happens to unsuspecting visiting teams.

**Bearden Gymnasium
Credit Author**

Built in 1927, this old gym has been home to the Bearden School Bears for some 80 plus years. And let me tell you, this old palace has been well maintained. It is sturdy, in good condition and is the pride of the school and community. Who knows, it might just last another eighty years! The court measures only a scant 30 x 60 feet. The court is arguably the smallest court and probably the oldest still in use in Oklahoma, which makes it a true bona-fide "crackerbox". And it's not a throwback gym. It is authentic, old school, real McCoy.

"Our biggest home court advantage is the half-court rule," explains McVeigh. Because of the short length of the court, three distinct lines are needed to determine half-court offensive play. The half-court line is the ten-second line to cross. You still have just ten seconds to cross it (like any other gym), but once crossed, a team isn't penalized for a back-court violation if they move beyond it while on offense. The reason being, there is so little court from half-court to baseline. Instead there are quarter-lines which are located parallel to each free-throw line. These become the "over and back" lines where an offense is penalized for a backcourt violation.

**Oldest gym in Oklahoma still in use--perhaps the smallest? ...
Credit: Author**

The floor is so short that all three circles (the center circle and two free throw circles) are just inches apart, which makes for quite an unusual looking layout.

The gym sports old fan shaped backboards (curved across the top rather than the standard rectangle version used today). It was a design popular decades ago. Also, the antiquated time and score clock is still in place. Funds which were raised for the clock was a long ago project of the senior class of 1953. Previously, they had used a chalkboard or hand-scored flip chart to keep score.

Bearden hosts an annual tournament and invites six schools to participate. McVeigh says the little gym can seat about 150 people at a time. "Because of space, ball teams and their fans have to stay outside until it is their time to come in and play. We run 'em in on shifts," he says.

Current superintendent Leon McVeigh is now in his 35th year at Bearden. He says, "Our 8th grade basketball tournament is the biggest thing that happens around here and playing it in an 80 year old gym is truly special. You can have your 18,000 seat arena. I'll take our standing-room-only 150 seats in a "band box" any day!"

Segregation?

Molson, Washington's gym was in a cramped basement. There were two sets of bleachers.... one side for the girls and one side for the boys. The practice wasn't to segregate the students. It was just that the girl's restroom was on one side and the boy's on the other, so the separate bleachers only made sense.

...Seattle P.I.

THE ROUND GYM

"New Providence, Iowa -- a unique name and a unique town! In recent years, the community has saved its most important resource…its round gym. Webster defines providence as 'looking to the future as a nation would in saving its resources.' The newly restored gym is the community's resource. The gym is as unique as the town's name; literally… a building in the round."

Round barns and round gyms! The genesis of the architectural designs for these two structures appears to be the same. Unfortunately, only a few round barns survive today and these are considered "an endangered species." Most round barns were built between 1900 and 1920, primarily in the Midwest. They have become relics of rural America. Most have outlived their usefulness and now teeter gently in the wind. Those that remain were targeted for restoration and eventually placed on the Historical Registry. Round gyms have followed the same path, except fewer were built, consequently, fewer to be found and studied.

It's interesting to learn why round barns were constructed. The answers may apply to the contruction of round gyms. Several theories have been offered, whether apocryphal, will be left to the reader. For example, in Oklahoma's tornado alley, the round barns were built to withstand strong winds. Their configuration forces the tornado to go over and around.

In Arcadia, Oklahoma, a round barn still stands after more than 109 years. The Shakers, a conservative religious sect located in mid-America, built the first round barns. They believed the circle interior to be the perfect shape, not allowing the devil to trap believers in the corners.

Studies have also shown roundness represents the most efficient use of space. An aerial view of a cow shows it to be wedge-shaped; thus, cows arranged around a circle with heads toward the center and the wide "business end" at the outer circumference, allows more cows to feed at one time. The concept sounds plausible. Another study suggests a round building is architecturally stronger than its rectangle counterpart. Also, round buildings offer greater convenience in storing and distributing feed.

Gymnasium with no corners …Credit: Kay Clampitt

Could the same architect who designed the round barns be the same person who designed and built the first round gym in New Providence, Iowa in 1927? Central Iowa may not be located in tornado alley, but on occasions this rural area experiences tornados. Parents should feel more comfortable, knowing the round gym provides safety for their loved ones. Again, the religious types cannot trap students in the corners.

Theoretically, a gym in the round holds more spectators, or at least allows more fans to be closer to the action. Today, more and more theaters and churches are being built in the round, confirming the folks in New Providence were ahead of their time.

The round dark brick structure located in New Providence is a landmark in central Iowa. It was built in 1927 by the New Deal Works Project

Administration, one of several programs set up by the federal government to provide jobs during the Depression. It was thought to be the state's first roundhouse-style gym. The two-story, double-wall building was constructed with 13" hollow tile blocks with a brick exterior. The entrance is on the ground level and is open to the full height of the building, with windows on 3 sides. On either side of the entryway are 2 wooden staircases which ascend to the gym and descend into the lunchroom. The upper floor holds the basketball court, stage and bleachers. The court is 72' by 38', an average size in the twenties, but very dimunitive for later years. A steel structure system carries the dome, about 35' at its highest point and requires no supporting pillars. Another way of describing the Round gym, picture Syracuse's Carrier Dome. All fans of college basketball know, the Dome has the largest seating capacity of any University gym in America. Can you visualize the Carrier Dome not with 49,000 spectators, but with 900! If you can, then you'll have a good picture of its little brother in New Providence.

Upon completion, the Round Gym was considered to be the finest gym in Iowa. Some critics of the round construction often made fun of it because of its uniqueness M.R. Whitehead, New Providence Class of '48 and an outstanding basketball player, said, "It was huge and hosted dozens of tournaments. Some of the fiercest high school rivalries were fought in the roundhouse. It was a showcase."

A typical Round Barn in Iowa" ... Credit to Maxheim Photography

The gym continued to host games until 1980 when consolidation came with nearby Eldora. New Providence lost its high school. "They took away our mascot, they took away our colors…. they took away everything," a saddened Whitehead lamented. Now the only round ball played in the Roundhouse are local pickup games. The high school teams are gone, but locals want assurance the unique gym doesn't go the way of six-on-six girls basketball.

It was a newcomer to New Providence who got the fund-raising effort into a nationwide spotlight. Jack Smith and partner Paul Dunn relocated their In-Line Skate business from California to the empty middle school. The nearby Roundhouse gym was one of the reasons they "fell in love" with the site, Smith said. "We're both basketball junkies, and I'm a history nut. I love old things, old cars, old buildings, and old people."

Smith called on a former college buddy, who works at *SPORTS ILLUSTRATED*, to give the fundraising campaign a jump-start. He was successful, as the magazine featured the gym, complete with a photo of about half the town's 250 residents standing at the front door.

The townspeople, who have a lifetime of memories, games, gym classes, plays, dances, and graduation ceremonies tied up in the Roundhouse, banded together and raised the needed funds. Continuing the effort, the townspeople formed a Renewal Community, Inc., a non-profit organization, dedicated to community improvements, historical preservation, and recreational activities in the New Providence community. After serving the community for 50 years as part of the school facility, the Roundhouse is now maintained by the Renewal Community. This gym may not host high school basketball games any time soon, but hardly a day goes by without some kind of activity. 4-H meetings, family and high school reunions, community club gatherings, birthday parties, pancake feeds and Drama in the Round, makes for a beehive of activity. This is one gymnasium that will never see its lights go out on Friday nights.

Jack Smith is credited with saving the Roundhouse for future generations to appreciate. "We don't think of it as saving a gym," says Smith. "What we're really saving is part of this town's history."

Small Gym, Championship Teams

Who said, "You need a spacious gym with all the amenities to develop championship teams?" Don't tell that to Oak Hill High School officials in Mouth of Wilson, Virginia. Their gym has a tile floor with a seating capacity of 400. Yet they have hardware representing several National High School Championships. Have you heard of Carmelo Anthony, Jerry Stackhouse, Ron Mercer and Rod Strickland? These are just a few of many NBA stars who have performed for Oak Hill.

THEY PLAYED IN DIRT BEFORE THEY PLAYED ON WOOD

"Randy Lukasiewicz is a nostalgic kind of guy. He loves his roots and organizes each year a reunion to celebrate events growing up in a small Midwest community. Classmates and teammates make an annual pilgrimage back to Farwell, Nebraska to learn more about their heritage to pass down to future generations. A former Farwell athlete, now a gifted writer, Randy writes about his early days and how Farwell athletes and coaches made an impression upon his life. Throw in successful basketball teams who performed under unusual circumstances and you have a recipe for an unbelievable story."

As a five year old, I grew accustomed to the sounds of shouting and the stomping of feet emulating from the high school gym, located just 125 steps from our front door. Despite the climatic conditions which can be severe on the plains of Nebraska, I often found my way to the front door of the most popular building in my home town. On this Friday night, a tall, athletic fellow in a letterman's jacket met me at the door and suggested on a night like this, "It may be better to stay home rather than brave the wintery conditions we're facing tonight." I replied, "I wouldn't miss this game for anything in the world." Today, reflecting back, I'm not sure a five year old even understood the magnitude of the evening. The gym was packed to the rafters and the streets were full of cars, pickups and a few buses. What was there about this game that was played in the uncomfortable dead of winter, attracting nearly 100 percent of its community members? Wouldn't it have been better to stay home, play with my match box toys, read a good book, or watch TV and munch on Dad's hot, buttered popcorn?

Welcome to Farwell, Nebraska, home of the Panthers. Located 120 miles west of Omaha, it was my hometown and your typical small village, with a unique history, issues and characters. It was originally settled two and one-half miles southwest of its present location, with many families of Polish descent. In the beginning, its name was Poznan, in honor of the same city in their homeland of Poland. The original site, laid out on a five-acre tract in lowlands, was okay for the railroad, but not well chosen, as it had a tendency to go under water when the stream came up. Flood waters and a disastrous fire caused the citizens to look for another site and in 1893 all remaining buildings of the old town were moved. Thus it became the "village on the hill." The name changed to Farwell, a Danish word meaning 'good-bye', said to signify a 'good-bye' to Posen.

This is a true story. I witnessed it just one-hundred feet away as a young, energetic kindergartner. Forty-five years later, happened upon the story…, five years later, I heard the story… today, I tell it!

1955 was a special year because I recall experiencing wonder, awe and mystery. The big, white double-front door of the Farwell Public School, where my Hardy Boys mind was like a dry sponge in a tub of water, was just 125 running feet away from my back porch.

I know how Lou Gehrig felt when he said on July 4th, 1939, "I consider myself the luckiest man on earth." As a scrawny lad at age five, in a town built on a hill with a population of one hundred and fifty, where I had free reign, or so I thought, what more was there to life in 1950? The three by five square block village, with its gullies, trees, and caves and where the vacant lots were our battleground and ball field, it was our whole world. I had a handful of kids in my class and my memories are varied and cherished.

It seemed like every night, and especially on weekends, whether at the school or uptown, the sights and sounds of cars, trucks, tractors, cats, dogs, and kids permeated the streets. I had no idea of what was going on, except excitement was in the air. What was going on? Were all kids everywhere as 'lucky' as I?

Darryl Krzycki and I got to be friends in one of the strangest ways. While thinking what activities to do during the Farwell Centennial in 1987, he suggested I should do a road race. With all the interest in walking and running, I heeded his advice and sponsored the Polish Marathon that lasted for several years.

A few years later, I moved to Omaha and crossed paths with Darryl. We laughed and prayed a lot. We spent quality time together as, we both loved our Cornhuskers and hometown of Farwell. During the heaviest snowstorm in my memory bank, Darryl went out to help his neighbors, the sort of thing you do when you are from a small town -- scoop snow. It was all too much. When he was finished, he dropped dead in his driveway. He really went HOME, if you know what I mean.

A few short days later, his family called and wanted me to have a couple boxes of his personal belongings. Delightfully and humbly, I accepted, not knowing what treasure I might find, but anxious because I knew Darryl loved sports, was Polish and liked to save, and was meticulous! I quickly opened the boxes and just by the smell, I knew I was on to something special. "Oh my God", I could not believe it! I was holding the only red and white men's town-team baseball uniform in existence from Farwell. The last time I saw this was probably one hot July, Sunday afternoon, forty-five years earlier on one of my heroes.

The search continued as I carefully paged through the brittle, neat, and carefully recorded home-made journal entries, photographs and statistics. I could not believe what I was reading. The "Farwell Five" had beaten rather handily most of the surrounding, larger schools. The girl's volleyball team went undefeated. The years were 1955 and 1956. I read on. The headlines on a tattered, yellow faded clipping, boldly stated, *"FARWELL GOES UNDEFEATED."* Ah-ha! Here it was! While I was a kindergartener, Darryl Krzycki was a senior and a member of the largest-ever Farwell graduating class of thirteen. He was a starter on the basketball team that lost only one game, which was to Holstein, at the Class E State Tournament in Lincoln. No wonder the Farwell streets and school gym rocked with excitement. No wonder my kindergarten year was memorable. It was not a dream or my imagination from forty-five years earlier. A big part of the mystery was solved, but not all of it. Success creates success and if that is so, where did it all begin? Could that big athlete who met me at the door in 1955 been the towering All-Stater, Paul Collison? To this day he still holds scoring records at Kearney State in Nebraska. Best known as the uncle of Nick, who starred at Kansas, drafted by the Seattle Sonics and now with the Oklahoma Thunder.

The MWA structure, the only building in town that could host a basketball practice ...Credit: Randy Lukasiewicz

The answer appeared in 2006, at another Farwell reunion. A local farmer, Jerry Hruza, proceeded to tell the story from the 1940's of a Farwell team that had no gym. Jerry was emphatic to point out that the boys had no indoor facility to practice or play, but yet beat the pants off everybody and then went on to state. They finally figured it out that the team beat everybody because they practiced and played outside and therefore, when they got inside they were used to running to 'keep warm'. A former player, Al Strelecki added, "We practiced outside the old high school where we could string up lights for our cold, freezing night practices." Teammate, Dan Dilla added "When we did play inside, it was at the M.W.A. Community Hall on Main St. where the court's width was three of us guys' arms out-stretched."

To me, it was like finding the 'Dead Sea Scrolls', as if I heard this revelation. It all made sense. Clearly, these driven, young men loved basketball so passionately they went to whatever means to play and compete. This pride and passion eventually was passed down to their children who became the heroes of the 1955-56 Season.

To this point, it was all stories, and nothing to document these 'gym-less wonders.' The fog of uncertainty disappeared when I found the following article from the St. Paul newspaper:

Phonograph-Herald, December 6, 2006, "Days Gone By, Sixty Years later."

Farwell, despite the fact they have no gym in which to practice or play home games, and barring illness or unforeseen circumstances, are headed for a great season. Local fans are dreaming of a possible Class D Championship. Coach M.L Vohland is in charge of Farwell's high-scoring team. The boys are able to keep in splendid physical condition by their practice on an outdoor court.

The team is composed of the same members as last year's quintet, which won third place in the Class D Tournament at Elba. They average six-foot in height, have plenty of speed and exceptional ball handling abilities, and each man is a potential scorer. The Panthers have already scored five straight victories, all by comfortable margins. The string of wins include two over Boeius, 41-21 and 47-17, one each over Dannnebrog 27-18, Rockville 80-5, and Ashton 75-17

Perhaps the story of the team that had no gym or hardwood floor and at times no coach, but yet somehow managed to go to State can be wrapped up by the big, towering center from 1949, Don Wolinski, who never moved away from the community. Now, standing at the microphone, on June 8th, 2006, and supported by crutches and unable to see, he reflected on his playing days by saying, "It takes more than a building and equipment to create a successful team. We didn't have a plush arena or a hardwood playing surface, not even an indoor court, but we had the intangibles: friendships, heart, pride, dedication to a cause, and all the things necessary for success. Support from a spirited community didn't hurt. The old school with its limited facilities didn't do a bad job in turning out responsible adults. Some of our classmates became Atomic and

Civil Engineers, and I'm proud of all who became teachers and nurses." He closed by saying, "It was kinda fun the way we did it…. and chasing all those prairie dogs!" Don's words and spirit lives on. He was buried Dec. 8, 2008 in the community where he grew up, lived, led as Mayor and Fire Chief, prayed, and loved. The distance from his back screen door to the big white, double-doors of Farwell High, the school he helped take to state, is only two hundred seventy-five feet.

Farwell Panthers – they played on dirt …Credit: Randy Lukasiewicz

I suppose my story is no different than scores of other small communities around America, with the exception, our heroes learned their game on the dirt surface behind the school, a hoop attached to a garage or one hanging from a barn. The hard surface would come later. The kind of venue really doesn't matter. The basketball court is unexcelled as a proving ground for America's youth. Within its boundaries lies a battlefield upon which physical skill, stamina, mental alertness, and moral development are fought for and won.

Maybe life back then wasn't so bad after all? Playing in the dirt and on the hardwood floor in the M.W.A. Hall? We certainly can't go back, but we can live today with the same values those young men had. At Farwell the baton has and is being passed down from generation to generation. The challenge is to move it forward without dropping it. The final score is but a small part of victory. And the game goes on and on and on and on…

Shooting the Rafters

Walford, Iowa had a home court in their American Legion Hall. Besides being small it had rafters running just about ten feet high and directly above the free throw lines. It was the home team's best defense until one of our players discovered that the braces that form a vee in at the center of the free throw line also provided an excellent sighting mechanism. His long two-handers through that vee turned the game around.

Contributed by A. Wayne Sterrett

BIG DREAMS ARE REALIZED IN SMALL TOWNS

"I've driven the highways and byways of Nevada, north to south and east to west. Other than Las Vegas and Reno, you won't see many populated areas, mostly small towns driven by mining and ranching interests. I'm thinking, surely there are scores of rural high schools that would have 'storybook' gyms. Fortunately, I met a young journalism student from the University of Nevada, Las Vegas, (Ben Rowley), who grew up in one of these villages and who also played a decent game of basketball. Ben recently earned a B.A. degree in Journalism and Media Studies and hopes one day to teach and coach at the high school level. He has masterfully crafted a chapter from his days growing up in Alamo. His narrative describes the ups and downs, the defeats and victories, the joys and sorrows that can only be lived out in small-town America. Ben captures the essence of the importance a small gym has upon a community."

I stared out the passenger-side window, taking in the golden scene. The sun sat low in the west, and yellow cottonwoods were scattered everywhere – casting shadows on miles of pasture. It was a late afternoon in early October 1998, and my mother and I were moments away from our new home. We had departed Hill Air Force Base, Utah that morning and made the seven-hour drive to join the roughly 1,000 inhabitants of Alamo, Nevada in the Pahranagat Valley. I still remember my anxiousness and my first attempts at pronouncing the name (PUH'-ran-uh-get), which is a Southern Paiute word meaning "valley of shining water." Pahranagat is an isolated, green oasis in the Mojave Desert, centrally located in sparsely-populated Lincoln County. It features a 40-mile long, one-mile wide, strip of gorgeous, green ranches that are nourished by a number of natural springs and are flanked by rugged, rocky hills on both sides.

My dad awaited us at our rental home in Yoppsville, a neighborhood built in the 1970's when Union Carbide workers commuted to tungsten yielding mines at Tempiute. Mom turned on to 1st Street. At the end of the town, which was just three blocks down the street, we saw a white, one-story building with an arched entryway. To the northwest, a church steeple peeked over modest homes and tall trees. The empty Alamo road took us past what I guessed was the high school and its little gym. "This is it?" I thought. "Where am I?"

Three-and-a-half years later, I was a senior, and it was the fourth quarter. I squatted in "triple-threat" position on the right wing, a few feet behind the three-point line. For a brief moment, I stared at the Lincoln County High defender. His Lynx were hanging tough, clawing back to within a point-or-two at that little gym in our own tournament. We didn't know much about the school, other than they were the Panther's longtime, cross-county rivals. That's all we needed. We yearned to beat them and were mad for a week if we lost.

The Lynx had bottled me up all game, implementing sideline traps every time I caught the ball. But the trap didn't come this time. I felt the anxiousness of the coach, my teammates and the home fans behind me. A quick burst of energy, and I flew passed the defender. His help came late, and I made a layup - plus a foul. The gym erupted. I turned around and looked at the coach. He was saying something, but I couldn't hear a word. That end of the floor in that little gym was the noisiest place in the world at that moment. I looked up at the ecstatic crowd, clenched my fists, and yelled with them.

Where I was, it turned out, was the greatest basketball atmosphere a boy could dream of. On winter weekends in Pahranagat Valley, you'll find half the community somewhere in the Silver State at an away game or jam-packed in the home gym.

The one I played in served Alamo's varsity teams from 1959 to 2005. The building's rectangular cinder block exterior won't drop your jaw. It's painted white with the school colors of blue and gold running around the bottom. The front wall features a painting of a large, black cat that looks ready to pounce and proudly states, "HOME OF THE PANTHERS." Inside, you find out why many called the place, according to current boys varsity head coach and former player Brian Higbee, "the loudest, most intimidating gym in the state of Nevada."

**Unique wooden banners showcase Alamo's successes ...
Credit: Ben Rowley**

The intimidation starts with wooden plaques. When opposing teams walked in, they were welcomed by the square, plywood banners hanging high on three of the walls. Former boys' basketball coach, Don Anhder, started them in 1985 when eleven stained and glossed beauties were mounted. The gym retired with forty plaques, all reading "State Champions." The banners honor baseball, basketball, track, volleyball, and wrestling teams, starting with the school's first title earned in 1950. By the late 90's, the top row was full, so the wall next to the main entrance sports a second string of glory.

The floor itself is only a few feet shorter than regulation size, but room beyond the hardwood is scarce. Opponents were crowded by either walls or fans on every side. Eight rows of bleachers border the north sideline with the front row sitting less than six feet from the court and team benches. The other sideline rests about three feet from the wall; ditto for the west baseline. The other baseline actually has about ten feet of room, but often the area was used as an overflow where spectators stood two rows deep.

Visiting opponents not only felt trapped, but trapped in a furnace. Coach Higbee recalls the heat being cranked for games. I never put it together until he said that, but I do recall cotton mouth coming awful quick playing in the home gym. Higbee said the Panthers were also aided by the west rim being about an inch shorter than the other. The feature wasn't created on purpose, and the Panther players and coaches didn't discuss it or count on it as an advantage. Yet it is true the home team always took that end in the second half, and rallies often occurred while the visitors scratched their heads to why their shots were suddenly falling short.

Home-court advantage culminated in the gymnasium's sheer loudness, which always made you feel like you were in more than a gym with eight rows of seats. "It looked like there were 10,000 of them, and it felt like it," Coach Higbee said. "It was so loud at times, it was like static." Screaming voices bounded off un-muted walls, and the tight confines allowed the sound to bounce quickly. "The fans were just right in your face," Higbee said. "Talk about an atmosphere for high school basketball – just incredible."

Of course, the key is that there were butts in the seats, and Alamo fans have never had an off year. The community cared long before the plaques. The valley *values* its youth. It *supports* its youth. It *stands up* for its youth. Often that support is misinterpreted by other schools. My co-worker played in the late 90's for The Meadows, a private school in northwest Las Vegas. The Panthers and his Mustangs enjoyed intense battles, but he always remembers being a little afraid when playing at Pahranagat Valley. "It was tiny and loud," he said. "And you felt like you might not get out of Alamo alive."

The support for the youth translates a little better outside the lines. For example, Coach Higbee's grandmother, Ev'y Higbee, has compiled a comprehensive history of the valley's schools and teams. As the stories contained in her brimming binders unfold, you discover that a different building carries the distinction of Alamo's first gymnasium. It turns out that white building my mom and I saw at the end of 1st Street was home to Alamo's high school students starting in 1936. The building was long-awaited, coming after a half-century of education evolution in Alamo. Before James Naismith invented basketball, one-room elementary schools dotted the valley in the settlements of Hiko, Crystal Springs, Ash Springs, Richardville, and Alamo. But for years, completing high school required uprooting to Lincoln County High in Panaca – 70 miles away, and many families made that sacrifice. Then in 1921, Alamo introduced a two-year high school, allowing students to stay home a little longer, but they still had to finish at Lincoln. In 1931, the valley's schools consolidated into one Alamo School District, and finally in 1933, Alamo was approved for a fully accredited, four-year program. In the fall of 1936, a brand new high school building was finished, complete with science and home economics rooms and the gymnasium.

Today, the building is subdivided into a courtroom and administrative offices for the Alamo Annex of Lincoln County, but back then it housed a similar atmosphere to its successor, though the dimensions were much smaller and even more cramped for the players. It was about two-thirds the width and half the length of a regulation court, and both baselines were inches from brick walls. Thankfully, there were pads under the baskets, because a drive to the hoop meant a slam into those walls, according Ed Hansen, who played for the Panthers in the late 40's. On both sides, rows of chairs went all the way to the sidelines. "When you took it out of bounds, you were standing on people's toes," he said.

But the marquee feature of the gym was low-hanging, wooden rafters, with beams perched not much higher than the hoops. Frequently, visiting players would forgetfully attempt long shots or passes that would ricochet off, inside, and between the rafters like a pinball. The beams were considered in play, so a mad scramble followed as players guessed what direction the ball would fall. "People would come play in that old cracker box and curse," Hansen said. Meanwhile, the "Alamo quintet," as reporters often called them, became pretty good at judging the rafters and shooting high arching shots over and through them and into the net. Not surprisingly, Mrs. Higbee said few teams ever beat the Panthers on their home floor, and Joe Higbee, her husband of 65 years and a former player from 1939 to 1943, recalls Dee Stewart especially being "a pretty good shot through those rafters."

The memories piled up, first in the "cracker box" for 23 years, then in the loud, cramped furnace for 46. There are thousands of stories deserving mention, which is one major problem with writing about Panther athletics. Anywhere you dig is a billion-dollar goldmine. But in all the stories, from every generation, are common themes.

First, the spirited, protective fans have always been there. When asked if they were as rowdy back then as they are today, Hansen just grinned. "They were worse."

Mrs. Higbee added it was always a challenge to keep the crowd in line. "They would get pretty excited."

That is more than an understatement. Why anybody would ever want to referee a game in Alamo is beyond me. You miss a call, you hear about it for a month. Don Anhder remembers several occasions when he had to escort the officials out of the building, getting them away from fans who wanted to have a few words. Anhder said he doubts the fans wanted to go to blows, but they surely were ready to share a spirited lesson on proper officiating.

Other gems are told on how Alamo teams faired away from their friendly confines. For the Panthers, an away game means at least a two-hour bus ride, and a trip to a northern town like Reno, where state tournaments are often held, is a seven-hour journey. Ed Hansen remembers one such trip during his senior year in 1949. The Panthers were in the state tournament in Reno, and Hansen recalls easily beating their semi-final opponent. That night the coach put the team up in an old downtown hotel, where traffic noise easily penetrated the walls. Instead of blocking out the noise and going to sleep, the boys stayed up all night shooting each other with water pistols. Hansen is disgusted as he tells the story now, but the next day the team was exhausted and got blown away in the championship game.

Mrs. Higbee recalls one of the few road trips she had as a girl's basketball player. The girls weren't privileged to go on many trips, especially during WWII when gas was scarce. However, in 1944 a friend of the school who played for Dixie College in St. George, Utah arranged for the Lady Panthers to come play both the high school and college. With gas rationed, each player brought her family's gas coupons. The team filled up the athletic bus (which was really about the size of a minivan) and then filled up 20 gas cans. They put the cans in the bus, put a blanket over them, and sat on them for the 332-mile round-trip. Thankfully, the bus didn't explode, and the Lady Panther's had a successful outing, beating the high school and giving the college players a run for their money.

Another theme has been a deep-seeded rivalry with Lincoln County. Joe Higbee's fondest basketball memory is beating Lincoln twice in 1943. His wife added "If we could just beat them, we didn't care." Hansen said there was so much animosity between the schools that they refused to play each other for years. The reason? There doesn't seem to be a valid one, other than they are the county's two schools, and Panaca has just as much history and pride as Alamo. Whatever the reasons, when the schools finally found the heart to play each other, it made for a fun brand of basketball. Everyone spoken with claims when the teams met, the venue was absolutely bursting with spectators. Through the years, congregational boundaries for The Church of Jesus Christ of Latter-day Saints required the communities, each heavily LDS, to worship together. This has probably simmered the rivalry down a tad, but things can still get heated. And it makes it more interesting to see the respective community members go after each other on Saturday, and then strive to love one another on Sunday.

One final theme has been the Panthers' championship success. Most of the state titles came starting in the late 70's. Alamo teams were almost always competitive despite constantly being one of the smallest schools in their division, but the Panthers would come up painfully short in the state playoffs. The first state title since 1953 came in 1979 under long-time coach and former player Vaughn Higbee. The coach happily stepped aside after a decade-and-a-half of struggling to reach the pinnacle. Rob Hansen, who played on that championship team, said "I've never seen a coach more happy in my life."

From there the floodgates opened. Boy's basketball earned titles in 1980, '81, '86, '91, '94 '98, and 2006. Today, it is tied for the 6th most state championships in Nevada history. The school has a well-oiled system of player development, starting with pee-wee, then the middle school program, and other sports have followed suit. The Panthers own 10 titles in girl's basketball (tied for 1st all-time), 12 in girl's volleyball (2nd), 11 in football (5th), three in girls track, one in boy's track, one in baseball, and numerous individual championships in track and wrestling.

This unprecedented string of success, coupled with the loud gym and spirited fans, has made Alamo the Nevada 1A equivalent of Duke University. It's a triumph in itself to defeat mighty Alamo. Last volleyball season, Lake Mead Christian Academy defeated the Lady Panther's for the private, Henderson school's first volleyball state title. Afterwards, an Eagles fan commented on Nevadapreps.com that "it is always good to see Alamo go down." A few years ago, a talented team achieved a rarity – beating the Panthers in their own gym. When the final buzzer sounded, a triumphant player knelt down at center court and kissed the floor.

Alamo H.S. in its heyday …Credit: Ben Rowley

I began this piece by sharing some of my memories moving to and playing for Alamo. At first, I cringed to do so, because the tradition, history, dedication, and camaraderie of the place are bigger than any one person, especially me. Yet I have an added perspective that I believe shows the greatest aspect of Pahranagat Valley's hardwoods and the community at large. In 7th and 8th grade, I was one of hundreds of serious ball players looking for that shot. I could play, but so could a lot of them. Tryouts were three days and consisted of two cuts. Both years I was a victim of the second cut. When I came to Pahranagat Valley in 9th grade, I found myself the starting point guard for the junior varsity squad after a two-hour tryout featuring zero cuts. The next year, I was on varsity and joined the battle for another one of those wooden plaques.

We won that Lincoln game, by the way. That night, I laid in bed thinking about my drive to the hoop and the crowd's reaction. Ringing in my ears was evidence it had actually happened. It was a boyhood dream realized, one that millions of young people reach for but so many can't grasp. I'm not just talking about making a big play and hearing the roar of the crowd. I'm talking about having the *opportunity*, the shot to put on a jersey, compete, and represent a community.

Thanks to Alamo, I found solace from the dog-eat-dog world of big-school athletics in the confines of a loud, little gym, and I take this opportunity to thank my parents for moving us to "the valley of shining water" and thank the community, which allowed me to bask in the game I love for four precious years.

It is a shame education so often is turned into an assembly line. It is a shame that our economic policies have squeezed rural communities. In doing so, America is hurting its own heart.

The 2005-2006 school year was the start of a new chapter for Pahranagat Valley High School. A new gym was completed and sits a hundred feet to the west of the old one. It dwarfs its predecessor. Inside, there are bleachers along both sidelines and plenty of room on every side of the floor. High on the walls, all the championships are accounted for. The banners are neatly divided by sport and are in a similar format, but the powers-that-be opted for blue and gold cloth instead of stained plywood. They look nice.

The new gym is pretty, and it has a lot more sitting and playing room. But we still remember that old gym. Vaughn Higbee said every time he walks in it, he has a million different thoughts. "I think about all those kids whose voices are still bouncing around in that old gym."

"It was bitter-sweet to leave such a great atmosphere to a bigger, nicer gym," said Coach Brian Higbee.

But such is progress, and memories have already started to accumulate on the shiny, new hardwood. I was leery of the new gym for a while, but then I attended a game last year when Alamo hosted Mountain View Christian, a private Las Vegas school. In the boy's JV game, an Alamo guard hit two free throws with just seconds left in overtime to seal a victory for the Panthers. It was loud.

In the girl's varsity game, two technical fouls were called on Mountain View. It was loud.

In the boy's varsity game, a Mountain View player made the go-ahead bucket with 10 seconds left. It was very loud.

And when there was 0.4 seconds left and the game all but over, both the home and visiting crowds chanted their team names at the top of their lungs. The noise level was close to what was provided in that old gym, now sitting quietly close by. That night, as I was writing about the games, I noticed a slight ringing in the ears.

I smiled. I knew there were kids staying awake that night thinking about the misses and the makes, proved by the ringing in their own ears. The community lives on, and with it another generation of dreams will be realized.

Not In My Gym, You Won't

Leonard, Missouri had a study hall/gymnasium with a ceiling just inches above the backboards which were mounted directy on the walls at either end of the playing area. I was officiating a game when a five-foot six-inch lad went down and dunked the basketball. The next time he got free for a lay-up, I was ready, getting ahead of the fast break. He took two steps up on the pad mounted on the wall so he could elevate for the dunk....whistle, and no basket.

Contributed by A. Wayne Sterrett

HOOSIER MADNESS

"Indiana is not considered a western, rural State, but when our topic is high school basketball, you'd better not leave the Hoosiers out of the equation. In selecting an Indiana high school for inclusion in the book, the challenge was to find one out of many, that best represents the state's passion for the game."

Each year between October and March, the entire state of Indiana submits to an affliction known as "Hoosier Hysteria." "This isn't a game, it's a religion," declares Howard Sharpe, who coached in the state for 45 years.

In the book, SPORTS and RECREATION FADS, Jerry Hoover is quoted, "If you went into the military and said you were from Indiana, they automatically told you to report to the gym. A lot of the guys were saved from KP, guard duty and getting their butts shot off because they were from Indiana."

Famed sportswriter Grantland Rice paid tribute to high School basketball in Indiana in his poem, *"Round My Indiana Homestead"*:

> *Now the basketballs are flying and they almost hide the sky,*
> *For each gym is full of players and each town is full of gyms,*
> *As a hundred thousand snipers shoot their goals with deadly glims.*

The Hoosier's passion for the game was first observed by basketball inventor, James Naismith. In 1925, he visited the state finals along with 15,000 screaming fans and later recalled, *"While basketball was invented in Massachusetts, the game really had its origin in Indiana."* Proof that Naismith was correct is documented by the fact, Abe Lincoln, politics, religion and sweet corn fall in line behind the game played with a round orange ball. It's the state where names like John Wooden, Bobby Plump, Damon Bailey, Oscar Robinson and Greg Oden are better known than the Governor. It's the state where high school kids become heroes and legends and their stories will go on forever. Drive down highway 58 that leads to Heltonville Elementary school, in the rolling hills of southern Indiana and find a limestone building that was once the high school, before it was swallowed up by consolidation. Enter the gym and there on the wall is a yellowed photo of the '54 Heltonville basketball team, the team that won the school's only sectional championship. Damon Bailey, Heltonville product, says "the photo is still there." The high school closed 20 years ago, but that team lives on in perpetuity in a small town of 500 souls.

Hoosier hysteria erupted in 1954, when Milan, a school of 160, defeated Muncie Central with an enrollment of 1600. Hollywood entered the scene and produced a movie that became a classic and remains today as one of Hollywood's most successful sport movies.

According to Wikepedia, nine of the nation's ten largest basketball arenas are found in Indiana. New Castle seats 9,314, followed by Anderson with 8996. Number ten on the list is Gary West with a capacity of 7,314. The bottom line…the Hoosiers are basketball crazy! They have a traditional love for the sport similar to the love of football in Texas and Minnesota's love for hockey. In his book, HOOSIERS, author Phillip M. Hoose writes, "In Hoosierland, the pulse of winter life is the high school team, the Sabbath is Friday night and the temple is your home gym." It truly is one of the state's most cherished traditions.

To find the gym in Indiana that best fits the criteria for inclusion in "Vanishing Hardwoods," was a daunting task. How can one locate the gym that best represents the passion and essence of basketball in the Hoosier state? This historic gym, besides having some architectural significance, must emanate a certain feel that is hard to explain or pin down. It's a spiritual phenomenon, feeling a place where people have been coming on Friday nights for decades. The physical structure ties the past to the present and on to the future. When you step into the relic, you feel honored to be there.

Could it be Newburgh? Fans that couldn't squeeze into the building often huddled under the windows to get play-by-play accounts from insiders perched in the rafters. I could write about Bruceville, where only bounce passes were possible when inbounding the ball, because the balcony hung over the court. How about the Ribeyre gym in New Harmony with a wall as the end line, and a court that measured only 68 feet? Someone compared the Huntingburg gym and its fans to the Indy 500, describing it as the "greatest spectacle in high school basketball." Or, perhaps Tyson Auditorium in Versailles, steeped in both atmospherics and history. What about the de facto home floor of the 1954 state champions Milan, Indians? If its walls could speak, what kind of a story would it tell? The list could go on and on.

Don Hamilton, a contributor to "HOOSIER TEMPLES", recommended Cannelton High School, located in south central Indiana, bordering Kentucky. It has a gym that's still standing and is rich in history. This community resisted consolidation and represents a small town that developed traditions, built around the school and its influence upon the community's cultural activities. George Padgitt, in his blog, SEEING SOUTHERN INDIANAS GREAT OLD GYMS, reinforced the selection of Cannelton, when he writes *"Towns like Cannelton are what really separate Indiana from the rest of the country in terms of high school basketball mystique."*

When the Cannelton gym was built in the early 20's, the school officials and the town fathers embraced a bold vision. The gym was designed to seat more spectators than the town's population. Undoubtedly, the school's administration understood the importance the gym would have in the small hamlet and for its future. To put it into a proper perspective, 70 years later when Cannelton built their new gym, its seating capacity was increased by only 100!

Cannelton, according to Wickipedia, is a city of 1,209 located along the Ohio River. The name was adopted in 1844 and was derived from the cannel coal once mined in the area. Cannelton is home to a former cotton mill, built in 1849, once the largest industrial building in the United States west of the Allegheny Mountains. It's now a National Historic Landmark.

The all-purpose Cannelton H.S. gym …Credit: Cannelton School District

The old gym can be found in the center of town and is still bursting with character. The playing floor is upstairs, in a building that once housed the firehouse, police station and town Hall. Padgitt remarks, *"If that does not speak to the importance of high school basketball in the community, then nothing does."*

Talk about home court advantage. Visiting teams had to adjust to the occasional fire alarm and police sirens. With the fire station on the ground floor, often on a response to an emergency, the trucks would fire up their diesel engines, resulting in the fumes drifting upstairs to the arena, which of course, affected the play. More than once, the game officials had to quickly respond by opening all the windows. Brian Garrett, the present Athletic Director, said, *"There was a benefit in having the firehouse close by. Most of the Firemen attended the home games and consequently, their response time was quick."*

The above-mentioned characteristics explain why many opposing coaches voiced their hesitation to play on Cannelton's court. Their excuse was that the gym wasn't large enough to seat their many fans. Garrett debunked their argument in saying, *"The new gym that opened in 1998 has only 100 additional seats and their real reason for not coming was that it was difficult for them to gain a win."*

An unusual happening resulted in another strange use of the gym. Joe Hafele, the Cannelton coach from 1950-'62, recalls a tragic accident that impacted the community and the gym. In 1960, a Lockheed Electra en route from Chicago to Miami went down in the Millstone section of Perry County, killing all 63 persons. *"It was an awful thing,"* remarked Hafele, *"the Pathologist put everything in rubber sacks and placed them on the gym floor, so the gym became a temporary morgue. The state police sealed off the facility, but they let me in because that's where my office was,"* the 79- year old Hafele said. *"The floor was old anyway and the chemicals they used ate it up even worse. When the court was replaced, they put in the same kind of parquet that was used at the Boston Garden, home of the Celtics."*

I began with a stanza taken from Grantland Rice's "Round My Indiana Homestead," and it would be appropriate to end the chapter with the poem's second stanza:.

> Old New York may have its subway with its famous
> Rum Row trust
> And old Finland with its Nurm runs our runners
> into dust
> But where candlelights are gleaming through the
> sycamores afar,
> Every son of Indiana shoots his basket like a star.

Cannelton's gym might have been the inspiration for Rice's memorable poem. I know it was a good choice as the gymnasium to represent Indiana's historical basketball venues. Every Hoosier would agree.

The dangers of playing on a stage

Wayne Sterett remembers when the gym floor was a stage at Paris, High School, in Iowa. Out-of-bounds on one end was a six-foot drop into the orchestra pit. Sterett said, "We were playing in a tournament and I saved the ball by jumping up, grabbing it, throwing it back to a teammate and then remembering, there's nothing under me up here, and unfortunately, for me, landed into a tuba player."

Wayne Sterrett, Muscatine, Iowa

Acknowledgements

I would like to offer my thanks to the following wonderful people, all of whom had a hand in the completion of this book (often behind the scenes).

- First, to my children, Jerry, Janis, Julie, Jill, and Jennifer for their encouragement and patience throughout the project.

- Dick Etulain, friend and prolific writer, gave me valuable input into the mechanics of writing and publishing. Heaven knows, I needed that!

- Phil Teakell, a former player of mine, and his lovely wife, Linda, took time from their busy schedule to travel the countryside with me throughout Eastern New Mexico, directing me to the many abandoned schools that are prevalent in that area.

- To Jeff Sharpton, talented graphic artist who designed the book's jacket and generously gave his time and effort to the project.

- Dr. Jerry Hull, retired Professor from Northwest Nazarene University, friend and colleague, spent countless hours in editing and proofing the manuscript.

- Finally, to all the individuals in the various states whom I interviewed: Paul Overly (Chester, Montana); Randy Lukasiewicz (Omaha, Nebraska); Steve Flores (Albuquerque, New Mexico); Francis Materi Wishek (North Dakota); Coach Marion Neill (Broaddus, Texas); Coach John Barnes (Aberdeen, Washington); LaVelle Cornwell (Ontario, Oregon); Ben Rowley (Las Vegas, Nevada); Elmer Reynolds (Martinsville, Indiana); Robin Kelsch (Augusta, Georgia); and Connie Okeson (Weskan, Kansas).

- Lastly, and most importantly, thanks to my lovely wife, Gwen …. I'll just say "for everything!"

Epilogue

The "Vanishing Hardwood" project began as a single state venture. I knew in my home state of Idaho there would be an abundance of old gyms to research. As the word spread about the book's progress, friends in neighboring Oregon encouraged me to add schools in Eastern Oregon. Their suggestion reaped some incredible storylines. Then, Eastern Washington came into the picture. Having coached in that area, I knew there were many small farming communities, who loved their basketball. I fondly remember attending their District basketball tournaments. I decided that after forty years, it would be fun to return to this unique environment. It wasn't a difficult decision to add Washington to the mix.

The title of the book evolved into "Vanishing Hardwoods in Northwest Country." I thought it had a nice ring to it.

The book format was short lived. The following winter, my wife and I took our annual trip to Tulsa to visit our grandchildren and watch our son's basketball team perform for Oral Roberts University. Eventually, Jerry became interested in the project. In his many recruiting trips around the state, he knew of many gyms that were old and historic. Many were built prior to World War II by the WPA. I was like the small kid in a toy store, as I roamed the state. I had a difficult time deciding which gym or two would be researched for the book.

Now that I extended the project into Middle America, it became obvious to include all the Western States. My work was cut out for me and I wasn't sure if I was up to it! I like challenges, so with my wife's blessing, I began the effort.

Two years later the manuscript is finished. It was a fun and worthy ride. Folk in small rural communities are "the salt of the earth." I met many wonderful people. The coaches and school employees were helpful, friendly and encouraging. Townspeople were eager to offer their input. Player's parents welcomed me into their homes. But it was the young people that I'll always remember. In these small towns, the kids border on the innocent. No pretense, unusually polite and respectful of their elders. I truly believe, they are products of their environment. It's sad to think that we might lose these kids as families migrate to the cities. It's happening faster than we think or would like to believe.

Unfortunately, for one reason or another, I wasn't successful in locating a gym in every western state. In Arizona three gyms were researched, believing at least one would provide a fascinating story. For example, Miami High School had a wonderful old gym that's still in good condition. Presently, it houses the City Library and a Sports Hall of Fame. Spending some time there in that historical community, I was unable to uncover a suitable storyline. The same held true for Tombstone, Arizona. Their stately old gym, which is no longer in use, is just down the street from the OK Corral. I was prepared to put a spin on a story, perhaps Wyatt Earp who grew up in Tombstone played for his high school, but found no records to verify he even attended school there. Just down the road in Bisbee, I located a most unique gym, a three story structure built into one of many hills in Arizona's storied community. The gym now serves as a storage facility for the city and the original scoreboard still attached on the wall is the only indication that basketball was once played in this vintage facility. I did my best to find a Bisbee native who could shed light on the gym's history, but was unsuccessful. I had similar experiences in Wyoming.

A disappointment was my inability to follow up on the many leads coming from individuals who submitted names of schools for inclusion in the book. The SOUTH DAKOTA MAGAZINE did a favor for me by running a short article asking for readers who knew of unique gyms to submit names. Twenty submissions came to my attention. Time and a lack of resources prevented from persuing each nomination. The fact that I didn't give each my full attention doesn't take away from my appreciation for their efforts.

During and since the completion of the project, I've received numerous communications regarding gyms in other states with stories that should be told. Others have asked why limit coverage only to the Western States? With such interest, I'm considering VANISHING HARDWOODS, part two, but I need the reader's help.

Here's the plan. We'll extend the coverage into all fifty states and the size of the school and community will not be a factor. ("Rural" will be stricken from the title) The other criteria will be the same. The book will be a collection of narratives written by individuals and open to novice or professional writers alike. Anyone who is interested in preserving vintage gyms and researching their histories are encouraged to participate.

If you are interested in receiving more information or submitting a narrative, please e-mail me at mfinkbeiner@cableone.net.

Contributors' Biographies

TOM BROKAW, *A small Town, a Tiny Gym, and a Hero*, is an American television journalist and author. Brokaw is best known as the former anchor and managing editor of *NBC Nightly News*. His last broadcast as anchor was on December 1, 2004, after which he was succeeded by Brian Williams. In the latter part of Brokaw's tenure, *NBC Nightly News* became the most watched cable or broadcast news program in the United States. Brokaw also hosted, wrote, and moderated special programs on a wide range of topics. He was recently, the interim moderator of NBC's *Meet the Press*, taking over following the death of Tim Russert. Throughout his career, he has been the recipient of numerous awards and honors.

He is the only person in NBC's history to host all three major NBC News programs in his long career: *The Today Show* in the 1970s, *NBC Nightly News* in the 1980s, 1990s and 2000s and, briefly, *Meet the Press* in 2008. Reprinted by permission of the author and the New York Times.

ROBIN KELSCH, *Panther's Pride*, was born in 1972 to Bill and Pauline Kelsch. He has resided in Augusta his entire life and graduated from Augusta High School in 1990. He is married to Angie and they have three children. He currently is Assistant Principal, Athletic director and Head Boys Basketbell Coach for Augusta Schools. He graduated from Northern Kentucky University with a Batchelors Degree in Physical Education and Health. Coach Kelsch received his Masters Degree in Instructional Leadership also from NKU. He just completed his 11th year as basketball coach, where he has already coached the Panther's to more victories than any other coach in school history. The chapter was written expressly for *VANISHING HARDWOODS*.

RANDY "LUKE" LUKASIEWICZ, *They Played in Dirt Before They played on Wood*, (Creighton, BSBA '72) has found peace, hope, personal and corporate healing via running, writing, photography and his Farwell FenceBusters sports collection of photographs and memorabilia. He has compiled his writing and a few photos in a publication "My Road." Other works have been published in the Bear Report, Best Poems and Poets of 2002, poetry.com, ephotograph.com and Teamonetickets.com. His interests, hobbies and loves include Nebraska history, small towns, Brown Park, the Lewis and Clark Expedition, the Neihardt Foundation as a Board member, the Chicago Bears and his three children Holly, Monika and Zachary.

Randy grew up right across the street from the Farwell Public School and was a newspaper boy to many a Farwell athlete and the well of stories and memories runs deep. The chapter was expressly written for VANISHING HARDWOODS.

KYLE NEDDENRIEP, *Some Old High School Gyms Find New Life*, is a sportswriter for the INDIANAPOLIS STAR, covering primarily high school sports. Before locating in Indiana in June of 2008, he worked for eight years at the SPRINGFIELD (MO) NEWS-LEADER, covering high schools and colleges. He is a 2000 graduate of Missouri State University with a bachelor's degree in Journalism.

Neddenriep's interest in old high school gyms began in the tiny town of Bradshaw, Nebraska, where his dad was a coach in the late 1970's and '80's. The school has since closed and like so many others around the country, the once-rollicking 1950's gym sits quiet, its future uncertain. The article was reprinted by permission of the author and the *Indystar.com*.

DALE REEDER, *Bearden's Bears Den is Mighty Cozy*, is a retired elementary school principal who as a lad in the fifties grew up playing on these old hardwood treasures. His father and six uncles were high school athletes, who all would later become basketball coaches. His dad began his basketball career on an outside dirt court before gyms were a part of the school campus. This family legacy provided Dale for much of his interest and inspiration in these small gyms. In retirement, Dale shared these experiences writing for Coachesaid.com, an Oklahoma sports website.

"Seeking out these old gyms and getting there was half the fun," said Reeder. "Traversing the winding narrow roads that followed the natural terrain of the land all seemed to lead to the doorsteps of the school… where the fun and good times began."

ELMER REYNOLDS, *John Wooden and the World's Largest High School Gym*, is a lifelong resident of Martinsville, Indiana. Reynolds writes a weekly column for the Hoosier- Times in Bloomington, on the subject

"Hometown Heroes." He calls Coach John Wooden, a close personal friend and was responsible for bringing Coach Wooden to Martinsville recently for a basketball reunion. His article was written expressly for *VANISHING HARDWOODS.*

BEN ROWLEY, *Big Dreams are Realized in Small Towns*, recently earned a B.A. in journalism and media studies from the University of Nevada, Las Vegas and is currently working on a M.Ed. at the university.

While studying journalism, Rowley covered high school sports for Nevadaprep.com and maintained a blog relating his experiences as he visited schools throughout Southern Nevada. Positive response to his work motivated him to launch his current project called The Nevada High School Report, which is a website publishing writing and other artistic and journalistic work from Nevada high school students.

Rowley is planning to teach high school English and journalism, coach basketball, write freelance, and continue in web publishing. He resides in Las Vegas with his wife and high school sweetheart, Robin, who is also pursuing an education degree. His article was written expressly for *VANISHING HARDWOODS.*

BRIAN D. STUCKY, *Home of a Ghost*, currently teaches art and photography in Gossel high school, Kansas. He has coached volleyball, basketball and track in addition to his teaching responsibilities. As an artist, Brian has exhibited at professional art shows, including the Mennonite World Conference. In 1993, he founded the unique Emil Kyn Memorial Art Gallery at Cossel high school. He is active in church and historical interests and has published articles and family genealogy books. His photography has been featured in the KANSAS magazine. The chapter was reprinted by permission of the author from his book, HALLOWED HARDWOOD, Vintage Basketball Gyms of Kansas.

RON VOSSLER, *Hardwood Glory, '60s Style*, of East Grand Forks, Minnesota, grew up at Wishek, N.D., and this article was originally published in the March 2000 edition of "North Dakota REC/RTC Magazine." Vossler, a free-lance writer and UND English professor, was the scriptwriter for the 1999 documentary, "The Germans from Russia: Children of the Steppe, Children of the Prairie," and scriptwriter and narrator for the 2000 documentary, "Schmeckfest: Food Traditions of the Germans from Russia," both produced by Prairie Public Broadcasting and the North Dakota State University Libraries, Fargo.) The chapter was reprinted by permission of the author.

NOTES

CHAPTER 6: BEDLAM IN A BANDBOX

Latimer, Clay; "Waxing Nostalgic," The Rocky Mountain News, 2/14/07.

CHAPTER 7: OLD BARN

Reeder, Dale; "Last Waltz slated for old gym in Welch," Coaches Aid, 1/20/05.

Eisenberg, John; "From 33rd St. to Camden Yards," "An Oral History of the Baltimore Orioles," Chapter 5, pg. 43.

Sooter, Kenneth; personal interview, March 10, 2007.

CHAPTER 8: WELCOME TO THE WEST

Bates, Samantha; "Monument's Past Remains," www.eastorgonian.info/main, 7/19/08.

Cornwell, LaVelle; personal interview, September 4, 2007.

CHAPTER 9: TALE OF 2 GYMS

Boehler, Karen; "Echos of Empty Gymnasiums," www.enchantment.coop, Roswell, 2008.

Flores, Steve; "Ghost Town Basketball," New Mexico Starline Printing, Albuquerque.

Herron, Gary: "Remember Pena Blanca H.S. Hoops," Rio Rancho Observer, Dec. 6, 2007.

Quist, H.L.; BULLDOGS FOREVER, Virtual Bookworm, publisher, 2004.

CHAPTER 10: LITTLE TOWN

Carpenter, Les; "March Madness: Foes Look past Nevada's Okeson at their Peril." Seattle Times, March 25, 2004.

Curtis, Jake; Nevada's Okeson is the talk of a little town in Kansas, www.sfgate.com, March 24, 2004.

Okeson, Connie: interview, March, 2007.

Stucky, Brian; Hallowed Hardwoods, Emma Creek Publishing, 2003.

CHAPTER 12: HOOSIERS, IT'S NOT

Barnes, John; interview. August, 2008.

Johnson, Carmen; "The Early Days of Saginaw," www.historicbrooklyn-tavern.

Sandsberry, Scott; "Hoosiers '08," *Yakima Herald-Republic*, 8/8/2008.

Sandsberry, Scott; "One Small Court," *Yakima Herald-Republic*, 8/8/2008.

CHAPTER 13: IMPROBABLE HEROES

Blakely, R.Joe; "The Bellfountain Giant Killers," *Bear Creek Press*. 2003.

Editorial; "Down Went Goliath," *Portland Oregonian*, March, 1937.

CHAPTER 15: TEAGLE'S LANDMARK

Fannin, Earl; "Broaddus Still Winning Big," Broaddus, March, 1977.

Heisler, Mark; "It's a Long Way from Broaddus to the Lakers," *L.A. Times*, January 14, 1992.

McMurray, Bill; BASKETBALL, Texas High School Sports Record book.

Neill, Marion; interview, October, 2008.

CHAPTER 16: CHANGING LANDSCAPE

Documentary Film; "Class C Basketball," Jason Lubke, producer.

Montana Hi-Lines: Travel Tips, www.bigskyfishing.com.

Overly, Paul; interview, *Liberty County Times*, Chester, MT, March, 2009.

Schlegal, Kisha; "Class C: Basketball, Identity and Loss in Rural Montana," New West-net. February 19, 2008.

Sheridan, Tom; "Class C Chronicles Hope's Last Shot," North County Times, September 18, 2008.

Skornogaski, Kim; "A Delicate Merger: Consolidation Schools Face Tough Transition," *Great Falls Tribune*, November 8, 2007.

CHAPTER 17: BEARDEN'S BEARS

McVeigh, Leon; interview. Supt. of Bearden Schools, February, 2007.

Reeder, Dale; "Bearden's Gym is Mighty Cozy," *Coaches Aid Magazine*, January 26, 2005.

CHAPTER 18: ROUND BALL

Clampett, Kay; interview, September, 2008.

Historical Registry; New Providence Roundhouse Gym, 1936.

Smith, Jack; interview, March, 2009.

CHAPTER 22: HOOSIER MADNESS

Hamilton, Don; HOOSIER TEMPLES, Bradley Publisher, 1993.

Hoose, Phillip; HOOSIERS, Random House, 1986.

Hoffman, Frank & Bailey, William; SPORTS and RECREATION FADS, Routledge, Publisher, 1991.

Mathews, Garret; "Gyms once truly multi-purpose," *Evansville Courier Press*, Dec. 17, 2007.

Mathews, Garret; "Odd-size gyms were once commonplace in high school hoops," *Evansville Courier Press*, Dec. 16, 2007.

Padgitt, George; "Seeing Southern Indiana's Great Old Gyms," Wabash College, www.wabash.edu.

Wickipedia; Cannelton, Indiana.